BURNING RUBBER

*A Memoir of
Travelling Wheelchairs in Asia*

KATHRYN LAROUCHE IMLER

Burning Rubber
Copyright © 2023 by Kathryn Larouche Imler

All rights reserved. No part of this publication may be reproduced, distributed, or transmitted in any form or by any means, including photocopying, recording, or other electronic or mechanical methods, without the prior written permission of the author, except in the case of brief quotations embodied in critical reviews and certain other non-commercial uses permitted by copyright law.

Some people's names have been changed.

Tellwell Talent
www.tellwell.ca

ISBN
978-0-2288-8804-8 (Hardcover)
978-0-2288-8803-1 (Paperback)
978-0-2288-8806-2 (eBook)

This book is dedicated to:

My children, Lenny, Anthony, Natalie
My husband, Bernie
And our five grandchildren, Jacob, Sam,
Michael, Penelope and Mila

And

To people all over the world suffering from poorly understood medical conditions like: Myalgic Encephalomyelitis, Fibromyalgia, Gulf War Syndrome, Long Covid, Multiple Chemical Sensitivities, Lyme Disease and many others.

TABLE OF CONTENTS

Chapter 1	The Man from Myanmar	1
Chapter 2	The Flight	7
Chapter 3	Stranded in Singapore	12
Chapter 4	Myanmar	19
Chapter 5	You are Home Mr. Mung	22
Chapter 6	Stranded Again	27
Chapter 7	A Purpose You Say?	33
Chapter 8	Cloudy Days	44
Chapter 9	The Slippery Slope	57
Chapter 10	A Medical Enigma	67
Chapter 11	A Few Good Men	75
Chapter 12	Life Keeps Moving Forward	87
Chapter 13	The Plan	91
Chapter 14	Taipei, Taiwan	94
Chapter 15	Ascension	98
Chapter 16	Bangkok	102
Chapter 17	Shopping Around	114
Chapter 18	A day from Hell	116
Chapter 19	Surin	123
Chapter 20	The Big Day	128
Chapter 21	Huay Thap Than	134
Chapter 22	The Elephant Festival	150

Chapter 23	Ubon Ratchathani (Lotus City)	155
Chapter 24	Paradise	172
Chapter 25	Hippocratic Oath	186
Chapter 26	Planning our next trip	194
Chapter 27	Thailand Adventure #2	197
Chapter 28	Korat Silk Factories	212
Chapter 29	The End is Near	217
Chapter 30	The Diagnosis	225
Chapter 31	Life as Kat	232

Appendix	263
About the Author	267

CHAPTER 1

The Man from Myanmar

If we all did the things we are capable of doing, we would literally astound ourselves.
— Thomas Edison

I had been working at a home care nursing company when they received an unusual call from an assurance company requesting a registered nurse with a visa to accompany a dying sailor home to Myanmar. This was at the height of the AIDS/HIV crisis in the mid-nineties and that seaman was in full blown AIDS mode.

I was the only RN available who had a passport, but I didn't have a visa. I had spoken to other nurses at our company who had worked as travel nurses and generally the experience was good. What could go wrong? How hard could it be sitting in an airplane next to a patient? Yes, indeed I was up for it.

The previous two days had been a whirlwind of planning a trip to Myanmar to take this man home. I didn't have to do much of anything — just show up at the airport with my passport and a carry-on bag.

I arrived at the airport via taxi; it was a beautiful, sunny day, unusual for February in Vancouver, BC. The air felt unseasonably warm. The near-by mountains of the North Shore were covered with snow, so picturesque. I had been in a bright mood myself, looking forward to the plane ride and some hot weather in Singapore, our stopover for one night, then two nights on the way back.

HIV/AIDS was in a sad state of affairs back then. Most people didn't understand how the virus was transmitted and although all kinds of people contracted HIV, which can lead to AIDS, homosexuals — in particular men — were blamed for the cause.

One of my brothers-in-law, since deceased (not from AIDS), was gay and we talked about the stigma of being homosexual and the fear of contracting HIV/AIDS. He lived with us, and my three children for a few years. For me and my children being gay was just being a person. I find what people don't understand, they fear, and fear causes distrust and anger which can lead to violence. Gay bashing continues to this day.

I didn't have a work visa for Myanmar, just a regular passport but somehow the assurance company got around that snag. They couldn't wait for a local nurse to get a work visa and I was only to be in Myanmar at the airport for a brief time to hand over my patient to his family. I must say his family and the assurance company must have pulled a lot of strings to get him home. A large amount of money was spent on this trip for this thirty-five year old ordinary class seaman. Although I believed he deserved to be with his family at the end of life, assurance and insurance companies are not usually quick to spend any kind of money, period. Especially for a young man dying of HIV/AIDS, there were not a lot of sympathetic people in the general public back then, let alone an assurance company.

The doors of the ambulance which brought my patient from the hospital on Vancouver Island opened. I peered into the back of the ambulance and stopped in my tracks. I can still picture myself, my jaw on the ground wondering if it was too late to run in the opposite direction. However, he was my patient and now my responsibility. I've had to face my fear many times in the past and I've often enjoyed the outcome, but certainly not every time. I was thinking this was one of those times.

What have I gotten myself into? I liked challenges and usually had the attitude that you only live once, as far as I knew, so I went for as many new experiences in life as possible.

I had never been really clear on the philosophical discussion of "Why am I here?" or "What's my purpose in life?" but I'd always been a caregiver, I figured that was my purpose. Of course, life often has other plans that can turn your life upside down and it did shortly after this "good will" trip.

The emergency medical technicians (EMTs) got my patient out of the ambulance and onto a wheelchair. My patient looked crazed; his long hair was severely matted and he had food particles stuck in his scant beard and moustache. He was still in hospital pajamas and they were filthy; I couldn't believe my eyes. My brain was going in several directions at the same time. *I can't do this,* was the primary thought I had, as well as several swear words like *Oh no, what am I going to do?* I felt totally unprepared for what I had thought this journey would be — what I had been led to believe it would be.

The next words out of my mouth to the EMT were "You've got to be kidding me". I had received the nursing report the previous day and had been told that:

a) The patient didn't speak English — no worries, I had plenty of experience working with patients in our large multi-cultural hospitals.
b) He wasn't on any medications — great I thought, I don't have to give injections or manage an IV. On the other hand he had been taking sleeping pills, but I wasn't concerned about that either.
c) He'd be ready in the morning for his pick up time — I was shocked that any hospital would release a patient unwashed, unshaven, UN-everything. He had been in hospital for over a month. There was no report from his primary nurse, or the assurance company's liaison, of the real physical and mental condition of this poor man.

The two EMTs jumped back into the ambulance and took off so quickly I could practically hear and smell the wheels burning. They didn't even help me and my patient inside the airport door. Again I felt like swearing, at whom I wasn't sure. The EMTs, the hospital, the nurses, the assurance company?

Thankfully, my patient and I were provided with first-class tickets. The first-class lounge of Singapore Airlines was close to the door we had entered. I picked up our tickets at the desk and the amazing staff had been forewarned about my patient and understood the situation. One of the desk women, without batting an eye at my strange Charlie Manson-looking patient, brought over a nice clean pair of pajamas, housecoat, socks, slippers and a comb. I was taken to the men's first-class bathroom and I had about ten minutes to get Mr. Mung (his name has been changed to protect his identity) sorted out.

I was close to panic mode when I assessed my patient's condition. He was such a mess I hardly knew where to begin. So with paper towels I cleaned his hands and face, and using the cheap plastic comb I took out most of his breakfast from his scraggly beard and hair. He was — or used to be — a handsome man from Myanmar.

A few men entered the men's room, took one look and walked back right out again. I can't say I blamed them but I needed to get my patient looking a tad better than when I received him. Plus the women's bathroom was busy.

All was looking up until Mr. Mung decided he needed to urinate. I kept trying to explain to him that he had a catheter, a condom-style one that was meant for travel, and his urine was collected in a bag. He wasn't having any of that; as he stood up from the wheelchair, the blanket covering him fell to the ground and he — without a grimace — ripped the catheter tape from his leg and chucked it all to the ground. Fortunately there was nothing in the bag or condom. He managed to urinate into the toilet without causing us both to fall on the floor. That sight may have been partly observed by a man needing to use the first-class bathroom. I had heard the door open and quickly close with a "Whoops!" and I can only imagine how the situation appeared. My patient urinating in a toilet with me hovering over him as he was very unsteady on his feet. Yes, I was sure that would startle anyone expecting to use the first-class bathroom to spruce up before the flight. At that point if anyone had said anything negative to me about the situation I would have lost it. I'm usually calm in an emergency; I've done CPR outside of the hospital setting more than once and have helped at accidents. After a few seconds of *Oh no!* and *Crap!* I shake my head and do what I've been trained to do.

Into the garbage went the catheter. *I can't think about that right now. If I do, I'll go crazy.* Words from *Gone with the Wind* were encouraging me onward. I could do this. All I had to do was put one foot in front of the other all the way to a village in Myanmar. It seemed so far away.

I could hear the announcement from the airline speaker urging all first class passengers to get on the plane. Somehow I got him in clean pajamas and back onto the wheelchair just as a stewardess came to help us get to the plane on time.

CHAPTER 2

The Flight

You must do the thing you think you cannot do.
— Eleanor Roosevelt

Whew. My head was spinning. We were seated in the first row of first-class passengers; however, Mr. Mung was in the middle section end seat while my seat was in the same row but right by the window. So, someone would be sitting between me and my patient. Great planning. However, once the gentleman (who would have sat next to me but across the narrow aisle from Mr. Mung) took one look at my patient he quickly asked to change seats, which was fine by me. I could sit in my seat for the next ten and a half hours and hope and pray Mr. Mung stayed in his. Our first stopover was Korea.

I wasn't sure if Mr. Mung had ever flown in a plane. I had no clue if he would become upset and agitated when the engines roared for take-off. I sure didn't know what I would do if at any time during the flight he became upset. I wasn't provided with any sedation or anti-anxiety medication for my patient. I could have used some too. I had a glass of wine with dinner later; after all it was free in first-class and staying calm was my priority. It would be hours yet before we landed in Korea.

Mr. Mung had the biggest smile on his face when we took off from Vancouver. There really aren't many places in the world that wow me as much as Vancouver. From the coastal mountains full of snow to the emerald ocean it's simply breathtaking.

If you're an outdoorsy type person like I was, there is always a sport or two you could do on the same day. You can ski in the morning and golf or cycle in the afternoon. The one downside of Vancouver and the Lower Mainland is the amount of rain we get, mostly from late October through to May or June and sometimes right to mid-July. But when it's a clear, warm day it's definitely hard to find a lovelier place to live or visit.

We moved to the outskirts of Vancouver when I was twelve years old, from eastern Canada where it generally snowed from Halloween to late March. One Christmas, in Ottawa Ontario, it didn't snow until Christmas Day, but it snowed and snowed and snowed so by the time we left dinner at my parents' friends' place it was a winter wonderland. I thought we wouldn't make it home, about a half an hour away, but my dad was an expert driver and got us home safe and sound.

Mr. Mung stayed in his seat for the most part. He was especially impressed with the two trays of dinner he received from the kind stewardesses. He ate and drank everything they gave him, no alcohol, but he liked the gravy so much he drank it straight from the container. He ate and ate. I had been told in the nursing report he hadn't been eating much and had lost significant weight. He was probably depressed, not having anyone to talk with for at least a month. I never found out whether he knew he was dying or not. The smile on his face was priceless and I felt so much better. I let out a big sigh and settled back in my seat.

We arrived in Korea. When the plane doors opened it was icy cold. Mr. Mung was ready to disembark but he understood my hand signals and sat back down again. The lay-over wasn't very long and soon enough the passengers were back on the plane, the ones flying to Singapore anyway.

It was a long journey and I was happy just to sit and relax, until Mr. Mung decided to get up. I jumped out of my seat not knowing what he was planning to do. He headed straight to the bathroom by the cockpit. Thankfully, I was instantly behind him, because he didn't close the door. One of the stewardesses closed the curtain to the first-class seats as Mr. Mung, who didn't have very good balance, proceeded to urinate all over the bathroom floor. As I learned, years later, in some Asian countries many public toilets are just a small drain hole in the floor. It's what he remembered I guess. He was trying to urinate into the toilet but with the plane swaying and dipping it was like he was spraying with an unruly garden hose.

I was helping Mr. Mung, who still had a smile on his face, back to his seat. In the meantime the ever so helpful, charming, and beautiful stewardess began cleaning the bathroom without gloves. My heart jumped in my mouth: a huge adrenaline rush had me leaping over seated passengers to the toilet to take over cleaning, not that I had gloves but he was my patient and my responsibility.

I felt there might be a general uprising of the first-class passengers, a mutiny if anyone discovered the actual diagnosis of my patient. At that time it was believed any contact with a HIV/AIDS person's body fluids put someone at high risk for contracting HIV. What if the kind stewardess had a cut on her finger? I was in a bit of a dilemma. I couldn't reveal my patient's diagnosis but how could I protect the kind stewardess who would not let me clean the bathroom after the shower of urine my patient sprayed?

How could I be a nurse without nursing supplies? No gloves, no catheter, no way of cleaning up spilt urine of an HIV/AIDS patient. What a nightmare. The stewardess almost shoved me out of the bathroom area. I kept saying "No! No! I must do it," but her English wasn't strong enough to understand the danger I was trying to convey. I couldn't blurt out "This man has AIDS." for more than one reason. Firstly, as I had been taught in medical ethics, never ever reveal a patient's diagnosis without consent; secondly, as I have mentioned, I was concerned about passengers finding out and panicking; and thirdly, we had travelled more than half-way across the Pacific from Vancouver to our stopover in Korea. Where would we go? There wasn't anywhere to drop us off except the Pacific Ocean; I wasn't keen for that to happen unless there was a beautiful tropical island where we could parachute onto a field. I've seen too many silly movies where the bad guy gets shoved off the plane without a parachute never to be seen again. They wouldn't dare. Quite obviously I had too much of an imagination. I blamed it on the stress.

By the time I had taken Mr. Mung back to his seat and had quickly debated in my mind what the hell to do, the bathroom floor was clean. I didn't even see if the stewardess had put gloves on.

Years later, after being splashed by a HIV positive woman's blood during delivery of her baby, I was tested for HIV and it was negative. I had repeated the test after I became chronically ill. Since the height of the HIV/AIDS crisis, research and education has shown it really isn't that easy to contract HIV from fluids other than blood and close repeated contact. I did think of this stewardess over the years and truly hoped she was OK. She didn't have any cuts that I could see on her hands. Still…

Mr. Mung settled into his seat and fell asleep for an hour or so. He watched movies and ate when awake. The three first-class passengers on the seats to his left didn't seem to mind him there. He was "behaving" well, unless he had to pee again.

The bathroom was cleaned by properly-gloved airport staff during our stopover in Korea. Hallelujah, things were looking up again. We only had six and a half hours to go! I settled back into my seat. There weren't any further problems, that is, until we reached Singapore.

CHAPTER 3

Stranded in Singapore

Don't expect too much from people: the less you expect the less disappointed you will be when they let you down.

— Unknown

We finally arrived in Singapore. I pushed my patient through the disabled line, all the time worrying they would look in my bag and find my package of gum. It's against the law to chew gum in Singapore. There were signs on the walls with a big X through a picture of gum, another important fact that nobody had mentioned to me. No medical supplies, no damn gum. I was beyond exhausted but the ordeal was nearly over, or so I thought.

We were to meet with the assurance company's staff in Singapore for an overnight stopover before heading out on the last leg of this journey to Myanmar. First, we had to pass through immigration. I followed the airport staff with Mr. Mung in the wheelchair through a throng of other passengers to a counter to show our passports. I kept thinking *What if they turn us away?* — not because I had gum, but due to my patient's condition. If Singapore had such strict rules to keep the city clean, what would happen if they found out about my HIV/AIDS patient?

The immigration area was packed with people, which may have helped get us through without too many questions.

I had to use my skills of subterfuge and talk my way around the question of what was wrong with Mr. Mung. I explained to the immigration clerk that I was a nurse hired to accompany this dying patient home to his family. I was sure by the look on this man's face we would be turned away and put on the next plane right back to Vancouver.

The immigration worker never directly asked what my patient's diagnosis was, or "Why is this man sick?" or anything where I would have to disclose Mr. Mung's HIV/AIDS diagnosis. I ccould say without a doubt I never would have let us into Singapore: one look at my patient with his ratty hair, pajamas, and a silly grin on his face would prompt me to investigate further but thankfully the immigration agent appeared too tired to really care. We were moving on to Myanmar the next day; actually it was already past midnight so we were leaving in a few hours.

We passed the "test" and off we rolled through the doors to the arrivals area to meet our driver to take us wherever we were staying overnight.

Nobody was there to pick us up. We waited and waited, and still nobody came. Soon all passengers were gone, then the airport staff. Mr. Mung was doing wheelies in his wheelchair. At least one of us was doing fine. It must have been the delightful containers of gravy he loved that gave him this energy. He was like a kid showing off on his new bike.

I found a pay phone near the exit to call the aassurance company's office contact in Singapore. No answer. No wonder, it was nearly 2:00 in the morning, Singapore time. I had lost track of what the time was back home.

Finally, I called my contact at the assurance office in Vancouver. I had no idea of the time in Vancouver, nor did I care. I was disheveled and exhausted and so was Mr. Mung, although he did seem quite content to play with the wheelchair. I knew he would have liked it if we found another one so we could race up the halls together. He was definitely in a good mood at 2:00 in the morning.

We waited until 3:00 in the morning for the driver to show up to take us to where we would stay overnight. Ah, the thought of a cool shower, a nice comfy bed and a seven-hour sleep. Well, the number of hours we actually had left to sleep had been reduced to four due to the delay in getting us out of the airport.

Outside the doors of the airport the air was warm and humid. I looked at the very old rickety ambulance van. How strange: I was expecting a taxi or regular car.

I really didn't care what this ambulance looked like as long as it took us to the hotel quickly and in one piece. We drove for fifteen minutes or so. Mr. Mung was lying on the ambulance stretcher looking comfortable and relaxed. I couldn't see much of anything out of the van window because of the darkness.

We turned into gated naval barracks. I wasn't sure why, as I had been thought we would be staying in a hotel, but we pulled up to an entrance and the driver got out.

The back door to the ambulance opened and a different man helped get the stretcher out. What? Where were they taking us? I was starting to feel uncomfortable.

The different man turned out to be a higher level assurance company manager who, thank goodness, spoke Burmese, as my patient did, as well as Malay (one of the official languages of Singapore), and very good English. I could have hugged him but propriety reigned, plus my underarms smelled bad. I don't remember this man's name. I was too overwhelmed by that point to think clearly.

We were in a military hospital and the doctor on call was meeting us in the room. The doctor, a short older man with grey hair, assessed my patient and was going to give him a sedative but considering we had to leave in four hours it would have knocked him out too long and it would be impossible for me to cope with him alone on the last leg of our journey. So we decided to see if Mr. Mung would settle himself to sleep.

The man from the assurance company, a middle-aged man, spoke to my patient in his own language then got him cleaned up and rested in a bedroom with two twin beds side by side, but no door for privacy.

I lay down on the other bed. As exhausted as I was, he was still my patient. Maybe I could catch a wink or two and recharge my batteries and face the remainder of the day later. We now had less than four hours to rest before getting up early to leave for the airport for our flight to Myanmar.

Mr. Mung fell instantly asleep. My adrenaline was still pumping and although thankful to get some rest lying down, I "surface slept" — waking every few minutes to see if all was well. I've never slept well; I was a single mom of teenagers at that point and I always had an ear open at night.

The driver and doctor had gone home but the assurance man sat in the other room on a couch until morning, occasionally looking into the bedroom-without-a-door where my patient and I rested.

Breakfast was brought in, some fruit and bread. Mr. Mung ate his down quickly but I just ate a banana. Hunger was not on my mind. Getting cleaned up was.

I asked the assurance man where I could shower. He pointed to another room, another room without a door. I couldn't believe it. Honestly, all I wanted was to get out of my sweaty, stinky clothes, put some deodorant on, and be human again. So that is what I did. I had a shower with my underpants on. I turned my back to the assurance man who sat right in the middle of the couch watching me with no sign of humility or embarrassment on his face. *Well screw you buddy, just DO NOT come anywhere near me or I'll snap!* I was close enough as it was.

I changed in a corner of the bathroom with a towel around me. I heard the front door open, and the driver had arrived. By the time they were back in the room, I was fully dressed. I had one carry-on with a few summer clothes and essentials.

The two men pushed the stretcher with Mr. Mung aboard. Out the door to the same old ambulance van we had arrived in very early that morning. It looked worse in the daylight. The tires were bald, probably melted on the steaming hot pavement.

I sat on the back bench close to Mr. Mung lying on the rickety stretcher. I hadn't really looked around the ambulance last night. The driver had a dozen Mr. Bobble heads suctioned onto the dashboard wobbling back and forth. Interesting. I then took a good look at the double-sided back doors held together by a coat hanger. The ambulance had no shock absorbers: it bounced up and down shaking the Mr. Bobble heads into a frenzy. Yes, I could see the attraction — or should I say distraction — for the driver.

The back doors were another issue. The doors were starting to part and stretch the wire. I kept having visions of the old movie where O. J. Simpson (yes, that infamous O. J. Simpson who may have gotten away with murder) when he was in one of the comedic *Naked Gun* or *Airplane* movies from the 1980s; the character was in an ambulance on a stretcher when the back doors flew open and O. J. and the stretcher went flying out onto and down the very hilly San Francisco streets.

This was not a movie though. I looked at the door again, and although not tightly closed, it didn't look about to fly open. I turned my head to distract myself and looked out the window at all the traffic. I could see dozens of taxis: small vehicles with advertising on an A-frame rack on top of the cars. Large signs, you really couldn't miss them. They read *Wear Condoms* in large letters, and *Protect yourself against HIV/AIDS* written below.

I started laughing under my breath. I was going crazy indeed. If poor Mr. Mung had read these signs on top of all the taxis before he signed up to be a sailor, he might have used condoms and not contracted HIV. I had a feeling he enlisted because he was gay. It wasn't exactly an accepted way of life in Myanmar.

Between the rattling of the back door, images of Mr. Mung rolling down the streets, and these taxi signs I started to laugh out loud and couldn't stop. Tears were rolling down my cheeks. Mr. Mung started laughing at me which made me laugh harder. We had a real good, stress-relieving laugh. The driver and Mr. Assurance Man must have thought we'd truly cracked. That was my diagnosis too. We weren't in Kansas anymore, so to speak, but I sure felt like we had landed in the middle of the poppy field in *The Wizard of Oz*.

CHAPTER 4

Myanmar

Whenever you think of giving up, remember what made you keep going until now.

— Unknown

We made it to the main airport and onto a much smaller plane bound for Rangoon (now called Yangon). On board were mostly media: men and women carrying camera bags and microphones over shoulders, writing and talking amongst themselves. The few others on board looked like business people. It did seem strange to me; why were so many journalists on board? What was going on that I didn't know about?

I should have read the history of Myanmar/Burma before I left; on second thought it, was just as well I didn't know, as in "What you don't know won't hurt you." I had less than forty-eight hours to get ready for this trip and Google didn't exist then.

The leadership in Myanmar has changed many times over hundreds of years. Myanmar has held a "democratic" type election every few years and Aung San Suu Kyi, the Nobel Peace prize winner in 1991, has won many times.

At various times the military has carried out coups and put Aung San Suu Kyi and her other compatriots in jail or under house arrest. Both parties, the democratic and the military, have been accused of allowing or supporting the genocide of the Rhohinga people, who are Muslims.

In 1998 the military was leading the country. A large group of students protested the military junta at the Yangon Institute of Technology. The military had held power for the previous two years. The universities had been closed down for those two years. A further 3000 students protested at a campus in the city of Yangon against the ruling junta. So, this was the country my patient was returning to, and I was entering.

Myanmar had bounced back and forth between ruling governments each with a different approach to rule. The country was poor and the military side was not open to US involvement in business.

Every person entering Myanmar at that time absolutely had to have a visa, not just a passport, and not many were approved. I didn't have a visa; there hadn't been time to apply for one. There was a war on.

There was a palpable excitement bubbling amongst the passengers. Many seemed to be greeting each other as acquaintances that hadn't seen each other for a while. My guess was two years.

Mr. Mung and I settled back in our seats and prepared for take-off. He seemed to be quite comfortable and cheery. I knew the journey to his home was nearly over. I was exhausted after being awake for thirty-two hours but

Mr. Mung was getting more and more excited recognizing his homeland.

The assurance company's primary liaison in Singapore had explained to him that I was a nurse and was accompanying him home to his family. I had no idea who he thought I may be. I was dressed in regular street clothes, not a uniform. No uniform, no gloves, no medical supplies — nada.

I couldn't see much out of the plane due to the fact Mr. Mung practically had his head out of the window. I didn't mind; I was so happy to see him happy. He wouldn't have much time left on this earth; any small thing to brighten his day was like watching a child at Christmas.

We landed in Rangoon (Yangon) airport but again we were to stay seated, this was just a brief stop on the way to another regional airport. This was difficult to explain with sign language to Mr. Mung. Again, nobody on the plane spoke his language. A bit strange, I thought, but we managed to get him back in his seat. The rest of the plane of reporters and businessmen departed, still upbeat and excited.

CHAPTER 5

You are Home Mr. Mung

Death is like going home.
— Chinese Proverb

Mr. Mung and I, two pilots, and two stewardesses were the only ones left on the plane after the departure of the journalists.

The stewardess opened a bottle of champagne. Well, mimosas. It was still before noon in Myanmar. Mr. Mung and I were each given one. He had a second mimosa but I didn't. I still had to be in one piece and coherent to pass over my patient to whomever was receiving him. I was tired and wired by then, way beyond exhaustion.

Mr. Mung wouldn't stay still in his seat. He kept popping up to look out the window and was trying to tell me what he saw. He was ecstatic. I couldn't help but feel incredibly happy too. Two people from very different cultures, different languages, and a world apart literally, we both had the same look of awe on our faces looking out that plane window.

It was a fairly short plane ride without other passengers which enabled me to get a good look at the countryside. It definitely was countryside, flying first over jungle-like territory densely packed with trees, and then flat land with huge fields of rice and other crops. The only visible roads were red clay dirt. I could see a few carts and wagons and people riding bicycles setting off clouds of red dust.

I didn't see any cars, trucks, or houses nearby. The plane started descending but I couldn't see the airport. But down we went. Mr. Mung was still popping up and down from his seat while the stewardess kept politely putting him back. He knew where he was and he was very excited. I'm sure when he got sick with HIV and ended up in the hospital far away from his birthplace; he must have thought he'd die there without family, friends, or anybody who spoke his language. He must have been very frightened. I didn't know how much he had been aware of his fatal diagnosis. I sincerely hoped somebody along his journey had explained to him that he was dying.

Finally the plane landed and even before the plane doors opened, Mr. Mung jumped up and stood right in front of the door and waited impatiently for it to open.

The door was finally opened and an official walked up the few stairs to the plane and was attempting to carry Mr. Mung back down. Mr. Mung wasn't having any of that and walked down the stairs on his own and sat in the wheelchair that was placed in front of the stairs. He was quickly wheeled out of my sight.

I was trying to follow them to discuss his medical condition with his doctor or nurse. A security guard wearing a yellow *longyi*, a rectangular cloth wrapped and tied around the waist, kept approaching me and trying to scan my body with a security wand. I was exhausted and overwhelmed: it felt like an intrusion on my body and after my last thirty-six or so hours I had had enough.

I kept trying to get past him to say goodbye to my patient. This man was only doing his job but the staff in this tiny airport knew I was a nurse accompanying a dying man home and after scanning me several times for weapons I started getting upset and kept swatting him back. Finally another official-type man told him to stand down.

Thank goodness. I'd had enough of a trial getting this kind, happy sailor home to his family to die. If I got tossed in the brink for being cranky so be it. It was a good thing I hadn't seen the 1999 movie *Brokedown Palace* at that point or I would not have been so flippant. I had even thrown my gum out, just in case. The thought of being chucked into jail was not my idea of a fun holiday.

Finally I was able to approach the other official men who were there to receive Mr. Mung. They too wore *longyi* and a few had white tunic shirts with medals.

One of these men was a handsome authoritative type, whom I assumed was Mr. Mung's father or uncle as they were hugging.

I was overwhelmed by this scene. Tears were rolling down my face partly from sadness knowing my patient was finally home with family, but also because he did not have much time left to enjoy life with them.

I didn't know if they knew his true diagnosis, but gay or not, HIV/AIDS or not, they welcomed him home with love and open arms. People in North America were still shunning the afflicted.

I never did get to say a proper goodbye to Mr. Mung, but he turned around and waved. I waved back. It broke my heart. Nurses try not to get attached in an emotional way with patients — it's too difficult if they should die — however, in my opinion one does get attached in the manner of caring for your patient. It's never only physical care. I had spent only some forty hours with Mr. Mung but we endured an arduous journey together. A little piece of my heart was left with him and his family.

I was led into the small barn-like airport that had a pretty painted facade of Asian-looking temple tops in various bright colours. The back of the airport looked just like the back of a barn. That's why I didn't see a "normal" looking airport on our approach. I really had no idea where in Myanmar we were. All I knew is that a hell of a lot of money had been spent getting Mr. Mung home to his family.

The very small first-class lounge was a stuffy room with a closed window and a Coke machine. How American. One of the stewardesses brought me a warmish Coke in an old-fashioned bottle. I didn't usually drink pop but it had some caffeine and that was good enough for me.

Soon enough we boarded the plane again. Now it was just me, the only passenger. The whole trip was like a strange dream I was caught up in. I had gone through so many emotions from the very beginning. How in the world were they able to get a passenger plane to drop us off on a teeny tiny airstrip in the middle of the jungle? Everything seemed so surreal.

Now that I was the only passenger on the plane, the stewardesses had found out that I was a nurse taking a dying patient home. Well, I felt like queen of the day. The beautiful stewardesses — and they were seemingly beautiful inside and out — kept bringing me mimosas, mind you the glasses were small. I had gone from 12 degrees Celsius in Vancouver to a humid 25 degrees in the morning hours in Myanmar. I was thirsty. I had three or four small glasses of champagne and orange juice. My stomach started burning. The only food I had eaten since the previous dinner on the plane was a banana in the morning. The mimosas kept coming; the stewardesses kept bringing them and bowing to me. I finally bowed back with my hands together saying "Thank you but no, and that was that.

At the time I thought the stewardesses were being a bit over gracious. I found out later Mr. Mung was the son of some high up government official from one side or the other of the ruling government of the day. Now that made sense.

CHAPTER 6

Stranded Again

Expect the unexpected even when it's expected.

We landed back in Singapore. I was relieved I had actually accomplished my goal of getting Mr. Mung back to his home and family. The hardest part really was over.

Like the previous night, I was to be picked up and taken to a hotel for a two-night stay. I was really looking forward to exploring a bit of Singapore while I had a chance. It seemed like a beautiful city.

However, just like the previous night, nobody showed up. I was so tired of these communication problems. One by one the pilots left, then the stewardesses from my flight left. Oh goodness, I had been forgotten again. One last stewardess who had been on our plane came by and recognized me. She inquired in broken English if I was waiting for a ride. Indeed I was; I explained to her I was expecting to be picked up, even though they were already an hour late.

The wonderful young woman offered to drive me to the hotel, but I had no idea which hotel I was booked in. She then gave me her address in case nobody showed up for me; at least I would have a place to stay. Wow, I was a total stranger really.

I called the assurance company representative again. I think both of us were tired of each other and upset at the communication problems between the two assurance companies in two different countries. He had been absolutely shocked the night before that I managed to get myself and Mr. Mung through immigration considering the diagnosis. I just smiled.

Finally the beat-up ambulance with the driver and bobble heads collected me and took me to a beautiful hotel downtown. By the time I was checked in I was so exhausted I could barely stand. I was going to change my sweaty clothes, have a shower and go out, but after my long, private, shower with a door that closed; I crawled into the nice, extremely comfortable hotel bed and dialled up room service. I ordered a bowl of Singapore noodles and a beer. I was starving but still couldn't finish the large bowl. The seafood in the noodles was tender and plentiful.

I fell asleep very quickly. After the beer I couldn't keep my eyes open any longer. *Aaaaagh*, I breathed a sigh of relief and looked forward to a good long sleep. It was 7:30 PM.

But why should something go smoothly when not much else on this trip had? The adjoining room was filled at midnight with very excitable, giggly girls. I tried everything to cut out the noise that disrupted my sleep.

I even stuck towels at the bottom of the adjoining door to block the noise but that didn't work at all. I even had earplugs in.

I finally called the front desk. The girls were just having fun, but between some of them running up and down the corridor and the others in the next room laughing loudly it had to stop. Apparently they were a sports team of some sort. Young girls are the same everywhere. I was missing my kids back home but I'd be there soon enough.

Shortly after my call everything was quiet again. I ended up sleeping twelve hours minus the midnight break. I took my time having another shower and changed into my sundress ready for the day. I ate breakfast in the hotel dining room and had a big plate of pancakes and bacon and real Canadian syrup.

It was time to venture out to explore what I could in my limited time. I received some directions and ideas where to go as a tourist, with only twenty four hours to see what I could in Singapore.

I did a lot of walking but after the amount of sitting I had done on planes the previous two days I was keen to stay upright. I had another long plane ride home the next day...

The city was immaculate. Not a bit of garbage anywhere. The very friendly people helped me find my way. I walked and walked. I saw a small shop on the second floor of a short building that advertised a tailor who custom made clothes. One of my girlfriends back home was a stewardess and flew to Singapore and Hong Kong frequently. She often brought home beautifully tailored clothes so I thought, *Why not have a couple of work suits and a dress made for me?*

I climbed the stairs hoping I wasn't being a bit crazy, but the tailor spoke English. He took my measurements and showed me different material to choose from. He asked me to come back at the end of the afternoon and my clothes would be ready. Amazing.

It was getting close to lunch so I stopped at an Italian restaurant and had a nice plate of spaghetti and a beer. There were several tourists eating already. I had a small table by the window and was happy to gaze at people as they walked by chit-chatting.

I was finally starting to unwind from the highly stressful previous days.

I finished my lunch and beer, I'll never forget that ice-cold beer that was served in an already dripping frozen glass; oh-so-thirst-quenching.

My next adventure was to find the Singapore Botanic Gardens and National Orchid Garden. I didn't have far to walk. My jaw dropped at the beauty of the park. There was a pond that was the same green as our glacier lakes in Canada. One side of the pond was surrounded by brightly coloured shades of green trees and grass. Everything seemed to glow like emeralds. An artist sat on a little stool near the pond with his wooden easel painting. It was the array of greens that stuck in my mind. I wanted to wrap myself in the cool colours.

I wandered through the gardens taking time to snap a few shots with my camera. It was a great camera, a fully manual Minolta which was so much easier to figure out than today's DSLRs.

I reached the National Orchid Garden and was instantly surrounded by the beauty and sweet fragrances of hundreds of orchids. I figured I was in heaven. There were so many varieties I lost count. Orchids have always been one of my favourite types of flowers and whenever I'm in a tropical country I'm on the lookout for the many varieties.

I was enjoying my afternoon completely. There was life and beauty here. I breathed the fragrant air deeply, not ever wanting to leave this park, but it was approaching late afternoon and I had to pick up my tailored clothes before the store closed. I couldn't get them in the morning. There wouldn't be time before I had to go back to the airport to return home.

I collected my inexpensive but beautifully tailored clothes and headed back to the hotel for a rest before dinner time.

By the time I was rested and showered again it was getting dark outside. I wanted to take some sunset photos and asked at the hotel desk if they thought it would be safe for me a single woman walking around at night. He assured me crime was almost non-existent because getting caught and having a hand chopped off was a very good deterrent. He was kidding right?

I stuck to the main sidewalks and got some sunset photos. Even though the surroundings were supposed to be safe, I always went with my gut feeling. It had gotten me out of trouble or potential trouble many times — that is IF I listened to my inner self.

It was time to eat again so back to the hotel I went and found a lounge that served light dinner. I sat by myself at a small table and watched an Asian movie. I was almost able to follow the story. There were a few businessmen seated having a snack and a drink. Everyone looked exhausted. I loved travelling but if I had to do it often for work I'd be exhausted too.

I went back to my room for a really good sleep and was up and ready by 10 am for my flight home.

To my surprise I was picked up at the hotel in a nice car driven by my voyeuristic assurance company representative. By this time I was very ready to get home. It was unfortunate to leave without seeing more of Singapore, especially the beach area. That would have been nice. I hoped to return some day for a holiday and have much more time to discover this beautiful country.

It was Valentine's Day and every woman was handed a red rose in the first-class lounge. That was a nice touch to end my journey.

After an hour stopover in Hong Kong I boarded another plane for the last leg home. I would arrive in the morning at the Vancouver international airport. To my surprise there were only a few people seated in the first-class area and I was able to lie down on the empty seats beside me and snooze the rest of the way home.

Ah, Vancouver I love you so.

CHAPTER 7

A Purpose You Say?

The purpose of life is to live it, to taste experience to the utmost, to reach out eagerly and without fear for newer and richer experience.
— Eleanor Roosevelt

I always thought I should have a purpose in life. I didn't have the best role-models for relationships or healthy family dynamics. Dad hid behind his newspaper and mom was a tad crazy and a lot selfish. My younger brother and I were adopted as babies.

I always felt I had a lot of love to give to many. I felt I understood people's pain and could offer encouragement and a shoulder to cry on. I don't like suffering and want it to go away whether it's my suffering, my children and grandchildren or the world in general. I have an extra empathy gene according to my DNA.

I had gone into nursing when I was eighteen and had only chosen that profession after a quick decision debating between secretarial or nursing schools. I wasn't proficient in typing and at least my nursing program would enable me to earn a decent salary for a woman. It would also get me out of the house sooner than becoming a teacher, the only other profession in which I was interested. Women my age (dinosaur) weren't exposed to many career choices in high school.

After graduation I inadvertently accepted a job on a gynecology ward but they neglected to say that it was the ward where women went to have abortions any time between six and twenty weeks. Some got through when they were more than twenty weeks pregnant. I'm a firm believer in a woman's right to choose, however, in my opinion abortions should not be done after fourteen weeks, when the procedure is much more complicated and risky. Of course with exceptions, it is not an easy topic or a decision. A lot of us rookie nurses quit at the same time after a year or two. The images haunted me for years, and still do. Another traumatic experience.

That just piled more shit onto my already complicated PTSD'd brain. I should have become a secretary. Less pay but a lot more peace of mind.

In later years, I recognized more of my strengths and realized I would like to have chosen teaching, psychology, or research in law or medicine.

In my late thirties I thought I may become a minister. As a young adult, I was dedicated, to attending a Mennonite Brethren church with my first husband and our kids.

It seems my "purpose in life" has changed direction many times in my life.

I got married too young and my purpose became doing my best to raise happy, well-rounded children. I had three children in my twenties and was divorced by the time I was thirty. I really wanted to have children because I was sure I'd be a better parent than my mom. I'd say the jury may be out on that, but I know they love me and all three have turned into amazing adults and parents. I'm so very proud of all of them.

My ex and I broke up the first time when my second son was three months old. My ex was an alcoholic, which I didn't really understand way back then. He didn't drink every day but when he drank he drank everything in sight until it was gone. We never kept booze in the house but considering he worked as a waiter and sommelier he was always around alcohol. He kept getting into trouble and at one point faced going to jail for breaking into the restaurant where he worked to take some booze. He eventually left the industry but the damage was done. Neither one of us were happy in the marriage so we separated.

Surprising everyone, he quit drinking and joined a church. He moved back in with us after I became very sick and had to have major surgery. Before I had the chance to restart birth control I was pregnant with our third child. I was ecstatic, especially when we found out we were having a girl after having two boys. A complete family.

Before my daughter was two years old my husband was having an affair; it was another blow to my self-esteem. We separated and divorced. He was a free man to start again, wherever and with whomever he pleased. He lived quite fine with a female dentist in Eastern Canada for many years, as I lay crying in my bed many nights because I had bounced a cheque at the grocery store, because the cupboard was literally bare, or because the electricity was turned off in our townhouse in late November because I was off work after a car accident (not my fault) and was waiting for financial assistance from my insurer. He didn't pay child support unless it was taken by the government whenever they caught up with him.

After I was divorced for a year or so I hired the next-door neighbour's teenager to babysit one evening a week after the kids were asleep so I could have some "me time" to decompress. I got a community pass for the pool because I was low-income so that helped off-set the cost of the babysitter.

After showing my pass to the two young women at the desk, they started mocking me as I walked away. Apparently, I was blight on society and there was no reason for them to see why I couldn't pay my own way. Their voices got louder as I walked shame-faced to the dressing room.

Total humiliation. I've never ever forgotten those cruel words. I had three young children and was newly separated from my husband. I was an emotional mess and after I figured out how to swim again, it was a good way to hide my tears. I must have cried buckets of salty water. I felt completely devastated: lower than a bug, as insignificant as a gnat.

I felt powerless in confrontation throughout my life. I go along to get along. When my kids were teens they often had free rein. I was always tired those years and standing up to teen boys is difficult. My oldest son liked to challenge me at times over silly things. Once he wanted the TV on and I had already said no. He came close to me, towering over me by nearly a foot. I stood my ground and won that silly battle but he left home when he was nearly eighteen and moved to Banff where he did a lot of learning about life on his own, good and bad, and met a lot of life-long friends.

There were a few good things that mom taught me and one was to stick up for myself and my brother. I'm better confronting strangers; I have nothing invested in them.

One year we lived in the basement suite of a friend who was also a single mom. There were only two bedrooms, one with a bunk bed for the two youngest kids and my oldest son had his own small room. I slept in a cubbyhole that I made in a nook near the furnace, which would go on with a bang every night during the cold months. I rarely slept. I was working twelve-hour days and nights. Single moms are zombies; it's amazing any of our kids make it to adulthood. Being a parent, single or not, is the hardest job in the world. Us single parents need a medal.

I had been very fortunate to find anywhere to live at that time. The rental market was at zero percent vacancy. I had looked and looked but there wasn't any safe place to rent to a single mom with three kids and a border collie.

I had put my name on a housing list and was eventually accepted into a co-op townhouse after a year of basement suite living. What a huge relief to have permanent and secure housing. I had to borrow money from a girlfriend for the shares one must purchase to get into a co-op — about $2000 for the place I was accepted in. I certainly didn't have any money and my parents turned down my request for a loan. It wasn't like they didn't have the money; they were quite willing to pay $20,000 each for a golf course membership. They had offered to take my eldest son golfing or have some lessons at their club. However, it was made clear "he would have to have the right clothes" and they made no mention of buying them for their first grandson. It was so hurtful. They knew I lived in a too-small basement suite and worked casual or on-call twelve-hour shifts at the hospital. I definitely lived pay cheque to pay cheque those years. It seemed once they deemed me an adult at age nineteen that was it; they were finished being parents.

There wasn't ever any monetary help from my parents. Mom literally sold me her old vacuum cleaner. She couldn't just give me anything except at Christmas and my birthday, when she'd buy something she really liked and was expensive and I would return it if there was a label from a store I recognized. She'd probably have a shit fit if she ever knew I did that.

They rarely took the kids for a weekend and I felt incredibly let down that they could not see or understand how difficult life was raising three children on my own on a part-time nursing salary for many years. I didn't work full-time days until my youngest was in her teens. Working part-time — actually three-quarter time — allowed me not to have to hire a nanny or have them put into day-care. I wanted to raise my kids, not have strangers do it.

During my years working on obstetrics and gynecology wards I had the ability to choose my own hours and days for the month. I generally got the shifts I asked for plus an extra half shift now and then. I worked day or evening shifts and thankfully no nights for the first several years. In the first few years, the schedule for nursing hours was based on eight hours shifts starting at 7 AM. I had a dependable young woman who lived five minutes from our place who was our babysitter/live-out nanny for a few years.

I loved obstetrics and worked with women and babies before, during and after birth. The majority of the births were normal with a very happy outcome after all the pain. A miracle.

I worked in a large obstetrical hospital where most women with pregnancy challenges went for expert care. I had grieved many of these women's losses and celebrated with a few when the outcome was positive on their next attempt.

For awhile I was the nurse people asked to bring a baby from the morgue to the mom and families. Nobody can do that very many times within a few months, to be with grieving families and not have their tragedy affect their own mental health. Working at a large obstetrical teaching hospital we were bound to be looking after all kinds of obstetrical situations and all kinds of women — a significant number from other countries. There was one woman who, after delivery, developed the flesh-eating disease or necrotizing fasciitis. It was horrifying watching this woman being literally eaten alive by these severe quick-acting bacteria. No known antibiotics were able to stop the deadly bacteria. She quickly became unconscious and died within a few days. Just one of the tragic stories we, as doctors and nurses, had to deal with too often. Her newborn would be raised without a mother.

A few other obstetrical cases stuck in my mind after all of these years. One new mother was very depressed. It was palpable when you walked into her room. She was a very quiet person but started to open up to me about her life at home in her small town up north. She was already a mother of four and didn't want any more children but her husband would not "allow" her to go on birth control. He sounded like a real domineering, asshole kind of a guy and this poor woman appeared to be broken. I referred her to the hospital social worker to see if there was any help available in her community for counselling or other assistance. The next day when I saw her again she was very upset at me for calling in the social worker. There are times in nursing you need to be a mind reader. She was terrified that her husband would find out. I hadn't thought of that and I should have asked her permission first but I felt horrible for this abused, tormented woman and had thought I did the right thing. I truly hoped she found some strength to ask someone, anyone for help. Years later, I pictured her and her kids driving down the highway with their hands folding up and down with the thumb across the palm signalling for help at the drivers behind.

Another time I looked after a young woman from a country in Africa where women were still subjected to female circumcision; it is an outlawed practice in most countries but many occur anyway. It's very hard to change the "rules" aka traditions in a developing country when women are up against domineering men in all aspects of their lives. This woman had been operated on after each child she bore to almost surgically close the vaginal opening. She had ripped from stem to stern trying to deliver this baby. Why her doctor didn't do a cesarean section to deliver that child was beyond me.

I felt a calling to be a midwife, I loved the process of pregnancy, and birth is miraculous for the most part. I started looking into the program but was injured during a night shift on a postpartum ward and had to stop working for nearly a year: my shoulder had been dislocated when a patient grabbed my arm as she fainted in the bathroom after giving birth. Eventually I had to have surgery.

I did not want to go back to working twelve-hour day and night shifts at a hospital. I could never sleep after a night shift and even on call I would have had to work some nights. I was happy if I got three to four hours of sleep when the kids left for school.

I had a huge scare in 1997 during my time working in the hospital. I had been sent for a sinus x-ray by my family doctor and a pea-sized tumour of some sort was found. My doctor sent it to a neurologist and the scans were repeated. I was terrified and tried to stay calm all the while attempting to keep my fear at bay.

I had finished the imaging and usually the technician comes out and tells you the imaging is good and that you would get results in a week or so. However, I heard them page the radiologist as I waited and waited on the stretcher, getting more and more anxious. Negative thoughts kept popping into my head, *Who would look after my kids?* They were still young; my daughter was just ten or eleven. I refused to leave the radiology room until somebody told me what was going on. I pleaded with them, told them I was an RN and a single mom, I needed to know. I could see the radiologist through the window where the technician took the images. It took some time but finally the radiologist came into the room just as I was about to go into a full-blown panic attack. He reassured me that the tumour was benign. Phew, I started breathing again.

I returned to the neurologist's office a week or two later and he reviewed the last brain scan. He was absolutely 100 percent positive the tumour was not benign. I was shocked. How could the radiologist have been so wrong to give me false hope? There wasn't anybody I knew that would be able to take on three young children and a dog and I surely did not want my ex-husband to raise them. He looked after the dog at his place once and the dog ran away and ventured all across town to get almost home before she got caught by the dog-nappers.

The neurologist got on the phone and spoke to the radiologist at the hospital. They argued back and forth for quite awhile and thankfully the radiologist's diagnosis was agreed upon. My tumour was definitely benign and I should have repeat scans in a year or two. That never happened. Ten years later when I began getting sick, the scan showed white matter similar to multiple sclerosis but not. A non-diagnosis.

My purpose shifted again. My kids were getting older and were more self-sufficient but after injuring my shoulder and my brain tumour scare I decided it was time to get a Monday to Friday nursing job. To be honest I didn't know they existed except in doctor's offices and

I knew the nurses there were not paid a hospital nursing salary.

I got a job as a home-care nursing supervisor and worked days only. Why had I not done this before? I actually felt like a human working day time Monday to Friday, and to my surprise the pay really was the same as working at the hospital. It was through this job that I had taken the dying patient back to his home in Myanmar.

For me, raising three kids on my own for eighteen years was a daily effort to maintain the mental and physical endurance to keep going and not implode.

I had double pneumonia the fall before I went to Myanmar. I was very sick for a few weeks and for a few years after that I had laryngitis and bronchitis every winter.

I was exhausted all the time, burnt out by forty.

CHAPTER 8

Cloudy Days

I was born under a cloud that has followed me all my life.

Mind you the sun has broken through many times. But that's life.

As in art, the term chiaroscuro, light and dark give the painting texture, form and power; so is life, without the darkness the light will never shine as bright and boldly.

— KI

My brother, Kevin and I were adopted as babies. Our parents had tried to get pregnant for five years with no success. It's interesting to note that most of my mother's friends that grew up together never got pregnant and all but one adopted babies. What was in their water?

I searched for decades for my "real" mother. I yearned to connect with someone with whom I could recognize myself. I eventually did. My half-sister found me after the adoption registry opened its files ten or twelve years ago.

When I met my half-sister in person for the first time, I looked into her eyes and found myself.

Up to then I felt I had no anchor, no mother to love. I felt disconnected, powerless, abused and broken.

Unfortunately our mom had already died around the time I had taken Mr. Mung home to Myanmar. I was born in Manitoba and always believed my birth mom still lived there. Mom had two other children after me. When I was a teenager I lived at home in Port Coquitlam my birth mom and family lived a half hour away. Isn't that the way the story goes?

I wondered if the reason my brother and I could never connect in a loving mother-child way with our adoptive mom and dad is because we weren't blood.

Kevin never wanted to meet his birth mom. He was happy in his misery, but he never found his answers at the bottom of the bottle. My brother and I had a long talk in our early twenties about "mother". I remember exchanging stories as we sipped our beer in the neighbourhood pub along with his wife who didn't drink much of anything ever, which enabled him to drink a lot of everything whenever.

He remembered things that mom did to me that I didn't remember, and visa versa. It was so painful exchanging stories. I hurt more for him than myself. I was supposed to take care of him. I failed. But I won't carry that burden — he chose the long suicide.

I often wonder what would have happened if my brother and I, along with his wife, had never had that meeting in the bar. How would I have felt if I only knew the story from my side? I remember when I started disliking mom, or at least didn't want to have anything to do with her; I was very young, just six years old. My brother was three. That's a long life living with a woman you have no love or respect for.

The assisted living place mom lives in is a constant source of complaint and disgust from her about people who use walkers or wheelchairs or have multiple medical issues. She just doesn't understand "how people can let themselves go like that." I keep reminding her that many times I have to use my walker or even wheelchair when we travel. "Oh" she says. Like she doesn't remember or care and those were years she was clear minded.

I know we had some good family times but unfortunately the hurtful memories stick in my brain longer. When we travelled or visited her wide range of friends and relatives my brother and I always felt we were on display. We had to just sit there visiting for an hour or two, never uttering a word unless spoken to. I never sat or stood straight enough for her. "Tuck your tummy in!" was a constant command from her. My body shape is very different from hers but her point of view is that everyone should look trim and fit like her. I used to be fit but my stomach has always been rounded, and darn sore from sucking it in constantly. My boobs are bigger too. I'm a mature woman who has lost her nice butt and gained more of a tummy. Speaking of boobs, I came out of the TV room at my brother's place one Christmas and there she was in the hallway telling me I looked like Dolly Parton. I was mortified. I'm a five foot nothing 110 pound woman with an Eastern European background. Just picture the lovely, old, short, round women with bandanas on their heads and carrying sheaves of wheat. Maybe not quite that extreme.

Now mom has dementia. Will my anger stop when she dies? Actually my anger has faded this past year. The past two years we have been in the Covid 19 pandemic and mom lives in an assisted living apartment that costs a fortune but keeps her busy every minute of the day. I haven't had to see her very often but the phone calls and visits are much more pleasant now that she doesn't have much to say due to the dementia and forgetfulness. There were many times in previous years when I would hold the receiver away from my ear so I didn't have to hear her go on and on about not one thing that interested me. She barely recognized the fact that I had been on disability for all the years I had been. She just wasn't interested. She might ask how I was doing but before I could answer completely she was onto another story about herself.

"Negativity bias" shows that our negative, harmful, or traumatic experiences in life hold more weight in our memories than positive experiences. Negative memories affect our perception of life more than positive events. Maybe one day I will sit down and make a list of the happy events of growing up. I need to find my gratitude again. We were well-fed, very well-dressed and always had a roof over our heads and an immaculate house. Life could have been worse but also could have been much better. Living in fear growing up takes a huge toll on one's psyche no matter how many positive events happen.

Mom revelled in the attention poured upon her because she was the perfect one and knew how to handle a crowd. She sucked the air out of a room. Everyone loved her except me, my deceased brother and his widow, my husband and our kids. There was an aunt or two who always thought she was a "spoiled princess." And now my brother is dead and I'm the only one left. I was so angry at him for dying. How dare he abandon me?

I didn't see a lot of my brother and family. We lived one hundred kilometres apart and I often wasn't feeling up to visiting unless it was Christmas. Life went on and I thought even if he had been drinking again, I didn't see it or hear about it. I thought he really had learned and was being sensible.

We received a call from my sister-in-law on Christmas day in the late afternoon five years ago now; it seems like yesterday. Kevin had had a stroke and was in ICU. Mom was staying with us that Christmas. My brother and I took turns having her at Christmas for a few nights. I had received a text from my brother a few days before telling me his youngest son was sick with the flu and he wasn't feeling well himself. I replied that we would bring mom out to our place instead and he could have some peace after his in-laws left on Christmas Eve; they celebrated together every year. His texts were sounding strange, like he had been drinking heavily and I was pissed off. Hadn't he learned? I figured he had been drinking again, sneaking booze when it appeared that he was only drinking non-alcoholic drinks. At my sixty-fifth birthday party he kept going to the bar and ordering alcohol; my husband Bernie saw him and told me about it later.

So I was mad when we texted and I didn't tell him that I loved him even though I suspected he was drinking heavily again. He was going on and on about how much mom had damaged and hurt him. He also said he had to have a drink before business meetings because he was a nervous wreck if he didn't. It was a confession of sorts. Then he died and my sister-in-law asked me to give the eulogy. I didn't know how to say no. What else is new?

I lost my way half-way through the eulogy. I was trying hard not to cry but the pages got blurry anyway. I did have some funny stories to tell. Kevin was good-looking and usually a good-humoured man. He knew how to work the room with friends at their parties. Even aside from the booze he was a comedian and could do impersonations that would have us in stitches laughing. He'd break out in comedy to try and keep mom in a good mood.

Bernie and I had seen the movie *Benjamin Button* starring Brad Pitt the night before the eulogy. I used the line from the movie: "You can be as mad as a mad dog at the way things went, you can curse the fates, shake your fist at God, but when it comes to the end, you have to let go." We were all mad as hell at his early, self-induced demise. But we had to let go.

It has taken five years to almost let go. The day that I stopped having a glass of wine every afternoon, as I had been doing every day since Kevin's death, I realized I didn't need it anymore to tamp down my anxiety over Kevin's death.

I remember the day mom and dad brought my brother home from the hospital. I remember the smell of boiling glass baby bottles and formula. One silly woman told me that I'd better be a good girl because mommy was very busy and I needed to stay out of the way. I was always a good girl. What was her problem?

My brother was quite the character when he was young. He was constantly losing his glasses which he had to wear from when he was just a couple of years old. One time they were found near the top of a tree. He used to rock himself asleep. The crib would bang on the wall. I felt I needed to protect him against mom but I was always too afraid.

One time my brother, who was maybe ten years old at the time, was on the floor with his head between the tub and toilet with mom on top, her hands around his shoulders and neck banging his head up and down. She was completely out of control again. We couldn't pull her off and I thought she would kill him.

I've never in my life been witness to such anger and violence before or since. I was terrified of her until just a few months ago when she sank far enough into dementia, the stage past anger. Now she's just plain confused. I'm sixty-five years old. She has held me hostage for many years. I tried to run away more than once, even as an adult, and my brother would plead for me to answer mom's hundreds of calls because she had started calling him at work hundreds of times during the six months I wouldn't talk to her after she threatened me with a knife. I had also run away when I was sixteen and stayed with our minister and family for several days. Although the minister listened to me about mom's erratic behaviour and anger, he had a meeting with mom and dad and she came across as a beautifully-dressed sane woman denying everything. Dad would just sit and not talk. So

I reluctantly returned home. My brother and I never had bruises or broken limbs; she would grab us by our neck or shoulders and shake and shake jumbling our fragile brains. We had bruises, but bruises you couldn't see.

My brother and I were quite good looking in our youth but still we had no self-esteem. To compound our situation, Dad was in the Air Force and we moved every three years during our elementary school days. Every province had a different way of teaching many subjects. We either felt behind or ahead of our classmates. My poor sleep and anxiety started then. I would dread going to a new school. We had to stand in front of the class of every new school we attended and introduce ourselves. We hated being put on display. I've never been able to form lasting friendships and until I met my current husband, most friends drifted away after a few years. Mind you Bernie and I moved four times in the first ten years. It's always been hard for me to make friends. I don't mind being a hermit to a certain extent.

When mom was in her eighties, after screaming at Dad when he had dementia, she admitted to me that she couldn't help it, meaning her out-of-control anger. That was the first and only time I heard her admit a fault.

Whatever happened to that woman in her youth? Her brothers were alcoholics; one had a family and died of alcohol-related illness in his early seventies. The other brother abused his wife, lost his driving license and family, and ended up living in grandma and grandpa's basement until his too-early death from alcohol abuse. Nobody thought grandpa drank, because grandma wouldn't allow alcohol in the house, but after grandma went to bed he would sit in his recliner with me on the couch watching evening TV and he would drink red wine from a big jug. Oh yes, he drank.

Everything had to be perfect according to mom, from how much tinsel to put on each Christmas tree branch to the shortbread cookies that had to be no more than one inch in diameter with a tiny piece of maraschino cherry on top. If it was too large it had to be done again. She had to maintain perfection or she'd blow up. She was always on the move, running away from herself. I bought her an Energizer Bunny for her ninetieth birthday. She gave it away.

When I was a teen she would trap me in her room and sit on me, straddling me so I couldn't get up. She would dig her fingers into my face to get rid of blackheads and pimples. Gross. I still have scars on my face and sunken cheeks. It never occurred to me that this wasn't normal family life until I started asking my friends about their parents. I was jealous.

My brother also had verbal abuse from our dad. Apparently my brother was lazy and stupid. He did have a hard time in school. I'm not sure why. After graduating high school, he had a great opportunity to move into the chemistry lab of a large petroleum business. He successfully completed two years of university and a compressed technology program, so he definitely was not a stupid kid. Learning challenges, definitely. Too many kids with learning disabilities are left feeling dumb and give up dreams of college or university. Some manage to find ways around their disabilities and succeed anyway.

Kevin and I were affected emotionally by mom from years of fear. We rarely knew when she might blow like Mount Vesuvius. There was no rhyme or reason to why or when she would go nuts. Once it was after a haircut she didn't like. She had a meltdown in the car when Dad and I picked her up. She was boo-hooing and screaming about her ruined hair. It looked like her usual cut to me, but really what did I know?

Another time, the last time she physically hurt us, was after she got home from work one late afternoon and found that the small cloth on the back of the toilet had been stained by a black magic marker that somebody had used on the bottom of the baby powder. Neither Kevin nor I knew what she was talking about, as neither one of us had marked the bottom of the container —it turned out his dopey friend had done it for some asinine reason that we'll never know. She kept getting angrier and angrier, her eyes beamed hot red, her body tensed like a rattler ready to strike, and strike she did, me first as I was closer. She slapped me across the face giving me a bruised eye and started shaking me by the shoulders again. Kevin grabbed her and she started hitting him but he pinned her against the wall by her neck and glared into her eyes and told her if she ever touched one of us again he'd kill her. That's when he took up drinking. I was nineteen, he was sixteen.

Kevin was always filled with guilt when it came to mom. He wanted to be good enough, and kept trying to please her when he was an adult. Mom expected a lot and we were supposed to conform even as adults. If I didn't call her once a week she would call me whining and ask angrily why I hadn't called. Everything was about her always. Did she not recognize that I worked shift work, was a single mom of three and generally didn't know what day of the week it was? She expected our family life to be perfect like the Cleavers. It was very difficult and exhausting trying to be perfect for her. After I got sick I didn't try as much to please her but Kevin and his wife took up her demands. They let her get away with a lot and she never understood how much it affected my brother's and wife's very busy schedules. Plus Kevin's wife had her own aging parents to care for.

During Kevin's "celebration of life" the minister said something about us being adopted. Now mom had always been up front about the fact we were adopted and all of her friends knew, but when our adoption was mentioned by the female chaplain mom popped up from her chair near the front and yelled "Why did she have to say that?" Mom started wailing. My nephews were devastated at her outburst and one nephew hated her even more from that moment on. Kevin's in-laws were mortified; they had always loved Kevin. Bernie was the knight in shining armour and took her out of the room until she calmed down. Strangely, mom never cries tears, ever. She boo-hoos quite loudly but never have I seen her really cry. It seems like she's been faking it at times. Maybe she wasn't allowed to cry when she was younger. I also believe there's been trauma of some sort as she grew up. She was sent to a family friend, for a year when she was five or six. I don't know if her brothers were sent away to some other place too or just her.

I spent twenty plus years with two different psychiatrists. I've been diagnosed with complex PTSD.

Complex and complicated; layer upon layer of hurt. My brother refused to go. Mom was diagnosed in absentia by my two psychiatrists, who heard my many stories over those twenty years, as probably having borderline personality disorder. She would have weeks of acting "normal" then out of the blue her anxiety would overwhelm her and she would blow with fierce anger: anyone in her way was in trouble. My brother and I lived in constant fear but masked it well. We would try to keep mom in a good mood by doing what she asked, like it or not. My brother became the comedian and kept us laughing during the periods between blowups, but we were always on guard for the next violent explosion. Her eyes would bulge and her whole body would turn stiff and she'd lash out. One time she had a butcher knife in her hand and turned it on me, waving it close to my face, when I commented that it looked dull and wouldn't cut the angel food cake we were having for dessert. That was the second time I tried to run away. After all the trauma I'd endured my first mental health diagnosis came shortly after the birth of my second son. I was put on antidepressants for a few months which made me feel like a zombie. This was forty years ago or so, and there are newer and better antidepressant choices now. I wasn't offered counselling although it was needed as my marriage was falling apart and I was scrambling desperately to make ends meet.

So my life was becoming more and more stressful never knowing if I'd have enough money for all the bills and groceries. Raising three beautiful children filled me with joy but it was often stressful to the max during those years.

I was sent to a psychiatrist because my depression was getting worse and worse. Depression is a dark and lonely uninhabited planet with deep agonizing pain you can't shake off. It's a dagger in your heart. Depression is intense grief, the loss of self.

I was put on different antidepressants over several years. Some didn't work for me, and some made me so hyper I wasn't able to sleep. Others that worked well would stop working after a couple of years. I saw the first psychiatrist off and on for ten years. I talked, he listened and somehow just having an ear listening to me helped so much. Plus the antidepressants. I've always considered taking antidepressants similar to diabetic taking insulin. Certain chemicals in the brain are not high enough and the antidepressants increase the necessary good chemicals while moderating others.

Counselling was an eye-opener. There were events in my life that I locked away in the recesses of my mind that came to light. I had been date-raped twice, interfered with by a moving-van employee when I was six, nearly raped in Hawaii and attacked by two men at a party. Fun times.

In later years I returned for counselling after becoming addicted to prescribed opioids. It turned out fortuitous to have had such an amazing addiction counsellor/psychiatrist. I learned a lot about the brain and pain, many ways to meditate, and a lot more about my mom, brother, and mental illness.

CHAPTER 9

The Slippery Slope

There are almost no sports within which mortal accidents are not a reality.

— Dietrich Mateschitz

I had been told by a few people over the years that I was very wise. I always thought that was interesting as I sure didn't see a lot of my life choices as having been wise. During my thirties and into my mid-forties I had the attitude "you only live once" (YOLO). I'd always been a bit of a tomboy when I was young. Finding me at the top of a tree having lunch was normal, as was splashing in the mud and picking up worms. After I got divorced I realized I missed doing outdoor activities and sports. I learned how to swim again; I hadn't gone since I was a kid, and I had to re-learn how to do it. I joined a sports club and re-started cycling, skiing and hiking as I had done in the past.

I loved sports of all kinds. I had grown up in Eastern Canada in Nova Scotia then Ottawa, Ontario. Every winter we had heaps of snow and we sledded and skated outdoors.

Moving to Vancouver, with its temperate weather, was both amazing and disappointing. I really, really missed snow at Christmastime. However, it seemed that every few winters including Christmastime it snowed in Vancouver and the Lower Mainland so I really couldn't complain. Plus with the local mountains covered in snow and Whistler a two-hour-drive away, I could find snow several months of the year.

Still, I prefer a nice glistening snowfall at Christmastime covering the trees, streets, lawns and the Christmas lights blinking through their white blankets. It's peaceful.

My craving for snow at Christmas must be from having snow each and every Christmas I had ever known since I was born. We also lived in Whitehorse, Yukon so a green Christmas does not feel like Christmas at all.

After my return from Myanmar I continued to ski and skate but I was having a very hard time turning left with either sport. I ignored it, thinking I had maybe strained a muscle.

I was no longer working at the home care nursing company. I was so tired and rundown. I needed a change and after my sick leave I decided to form my own home care nursing company with two partners. It had been a dream of mine for years. We were bought out after a good run of two or three years. I had faced my fears and anxieties many times running this company.

In early April, just a month and a half after my return from Myanmar I started having double vision and was sent to the emergency room at Vancouver General Hospital to see the head ophthalmologist. I was given a diagnosis of sixth nerve palsy. It took at least six weeks to reverse itself so I couldn't drive or go out of the house without one eye closed to straighten my vision. I didn't go far. I would get dizzy. Fortunately, our home care company was in the early stages of development and I was able to see without double vision inside a room. I had a lot of headaches.

That summer I had a very bad fall off my bike when cycling on Saltspring Island, part of the Gulf Islands between the mainland and Vancouver Island. Somehow, a hornet fell down my cycling shirt and into my sports bra. It began stinging and biting me on the chest. It felt like I was on fire. I kept swatting at my chest trying to stop the pain while at the same time trying to get my right foot out of the new clips on my pedals. I lost my balance and fell towards the traffic-congested street full of slow moving cars on the way to the ferry to go back to the mainland. Thankfully nobody ran me over. A few kind people got out of their cars to help me and my cycling buddy realized I was no longer behind and also came to my rescue.

I assessed myself for broken limbs: I was scraped up and felt shattered but somehow got back on my bike and cycled slowly downhill and onto the ferry then straight home to bed. When I got changed at home the hornet was still in my sports bra, dead. I stomped on it just in case it had nine or a hundred lives. I counted seventeen stings and bites on my right chest.

The following morning I couldn't move my legs. I had to get my poor daughter to help me onto a bucket to pee. Poor child I probably damaged her for life. But she was a trooper and helped me out. I called my girlfriend, another RN who came to take me to the emergency room at Vancouver General Hospital again. I was becoming a repeat customer. Did I collect points?

After an MRI and bone scan of my right foot it was determined to be all soft tissue injuries, which can take much longer to heal than some fractures.

I had a huge hematoma (bruise) covering my lower back from one side to the other. No wonder I couldn't walk with all the bleeding and inflammation. After I was able to stand up I had to walk with a cane for five months or so, my balance was not steady, my right leg felt weak And I couldn't pull my foot up off the ground. The first few months after my vision problems and my horrible fall I was often winded, finding it very hard to climb stairs, let alone cycle or ski. I must have picked up something in Myanmar, a virus or something. My symptoms made no sense and nothing was showing up on the myriad blood and other diagnostic tests. After several months it seemed I had recovered well enough to join the workforce full time again. I brushed the whole experience off. I certainly knew that not everything in medicine was as clear as many doctors liked to think.

I took a temporary job on a Caribbean cruise ship where I only had one or two, two to four hour shifts a day for ten days. The rest of the time was my own, to enjoy the islands for a good part of the day, or if I had a shift when the boat was docked I was notified by pager if needed. I never received any pages because when we docked at the many island stops all the passengers disembarked so my job entailed sitting by the pool awaiting non-existent pages. Loved it.

During the evening when not working I was able to see the shows or sit in the piano bar. What a life, but I couldn't do it long-term as I still had to pay rent at home and feed the kids, cats and dog. Somehow after our first dog died we ended up with two cats and another dog. I'm such a pushover.

It was a great paid holiday. This occurred during the years when the Norovirus started appearing on cruise ships which made passengers very sick and spread like wildfire. Thankfully, I didn't get sick and decided it would be a bad idea for me to continue working on cruise ships as I had been getting sick easily. I had H-pylori, giardiasis, a kidney infection, and bronchitis pneumonia within a couple of years. What had happened to my previous good immunity?

After recuperating from my bike accident, I continued playing softball, swimming, and going on hikes or cycling. I certainly wasn't back to my previous ability but figured I'd get stronger as time went by: that is, until the next accident. *You've got to be kidding me!* My life was definitely off-balance but after lots of investigation no reason was found for my weak right leg. I attended physiotherapy but never improved enough to play baseball the following summer.

I did join my friends on a weekend softball tournament in the interior of BC but was just planning on keeping score. I didn't think I'd be able to run as fast as I usually could and was happy to enjoy watching the games. But on Sunday of the long-weekend tournament, a team that was getting close to playing for first place on Monday didn't have enough women left to play the next game. It was a mixed league and you had to have so many women to keep the teams even. I played well and the team won. It sure felt good to play again.

The next day I was limping badly again and had an interesting time driving home, unable to lift my right leg and foot on and off the gas and brake pedal. I made it back and attended physiotherapy again.

My leg continued to feel a bit weaker than before but no cause could be found so I just carried on with work and played my sports the best I could. I was beginning to feel like Eeyore from *Winnie the Pooh*, walking around with a black cloud over my head.

That winter I felt I was fully healed after the bike accident and went on what turned out to be a disastrous ski trip. I had just sold the nursing home care business and had some time off before I started my new job as an Assistant Director of Care on a medical and dementia ward.

I had recently broken up with someone I dated for close to two years and was looking forward to the ski trip with some old friends. Nobody had to drive. About thirty of us went on a bus to one of the mountains in the interior of BC. Somehow the bus driver turned left instead of right on the highway and by the time we turned around it was after 11 PM when we were dropped off at the ski hill hotel.

We all had a bite to eat and a beer in the bar which had been kept open a bit late for us.

In the morning the mountain was socked in with heavy fog and rain. The lifts were closed but would hopefully open by noon. It was a very small ski lodge and there wasn't a lot to do aside from skiing, eating, and drinking. Most of us liked to "earn" our après-ski beer after participating first in the skiing or hiking or what-have-you. No set rule though, I'm sure.

The fog lifted at the top of the mountain a couple of hours later and the main chair lift opened. There were only a few of us who decided that we had paid to ski so we should at least try to have a few runs until the lifts closed again at 3:30. I had not skied at this resort before.

A girl I was rooming with and I decided to give the mountains a try. This was her first time on this mountain too. It had stopped raining. We got on the lift and by the time we reached the top the fog had enshrouded the mountains again. The fog was so dense we couldn't see each other, let alone where the start of the run was located. If you have never skied, the ski runs are usually well-marked with green for beginner, blue for intermediate, and black for experts.

We looked around and couldn't find any markers as to what type of run we were facing on the right side of the chair lift. Black or advanced/expert runs can have tricky moguls and I certainly wasn't an expert. I was always content skiing blue or intermediate runs.

We inched our way to the top of the run to see what we were getting into. The fog was so dense it was going to be a gamble but we thought it was more likely to be a blue run beside the only chair running. My friend started downhill slowly. I lost sight of her immediately as I tried to follow. It was a black run. *Shit!* I hit an unseen icy mogul near the top. I lost control and fell face forward. The hill was so icy I couldn't control the speed or direction I was sliding. I had on a one-piece ski suit which did nothing but make a flat slippery surface to fly down the icy slope. I bounced over moguls and picked up speed, headed straight for the huge cement truncheons that held up the ski chair lifts.

I still had one ski still attached to my right foot and I couldn't shake it off. I had no idea where the other ski or my poles were. I pushed my arms straight out in front of me and tried to slow myself down by digging my hands into the ice as there was not much snow. I had visions of all the poor souls who have died in a similar manner, crashing into tree wells unable to turn out of the way in time.

Well tough shit, I thought, *I'm not going to die.* I refused to die just when my life was getting better. Although my kids were older, I wasn't about to make them orphans.

I don't know how I finally stopped, but I was really close to the cement pole. My girlfriend and another skier caught up to me with my other ski and poles. They helped me down the rest of the run. The chair lifts had been shut down shortly after we had reached the top.

That was the last time I ever skied.

Again, I had soft tissue injuries but had to suck it up because I was starting my new job as an Assistant Director of Care. Good job, good pay, better hours, things were looking up. But I had to endure my pain and keep moving. Being active is usually a good way to strengthen muscles, but I hadn't had enough time to heal them first before zooming around wards again.

I enjoyed my job but it was a very busy position and I was often power-walking around the wards where the hallways formed a large square. There was a lot of territory for me to get around every day. But I liked to be busy and keep moving.

I didn't play baseball any longer, nor did I ski, but I'd always swam forty-two lengths at least once a week, usually twice depending on my job and time of year. I also started a dance class one evening a week. I'd leave my job, grab a bite to eat at home and drive downtown for my dance class. I was turning into my mother: busy, busy, and busy.

My right leg started misbehaving again. After swimming I would limp after I got out of the pool. My dance class wasn't going well because I had to drag my right leg around. I was worried. What was going on? I seemed to be falling apart physically again.

I went to a new physiotherapist close to where I worked who put large sponges with suction on my back, legs, and stomach. The sponges were attached to wires on a machine. It seemed strange to me. I had had TENS therapy before but the unit and pads were small. The physiotherapist hooked me up, turned on the machine, dimmed the lights and left saying he would be back to check me in ten to fifteen minutes.

It had been more than fifteen minutes and nobody came. I was getting pretty sore. I couldn't reach the machine to turn the level of stimulation down. I wasn't given a bell to ring to call anyone for help. This was really getting painful and I started shouting out for help. Nobody came. I was in a room at the back of the clinic. I began to feel I was in the Twilight Zone, captured and tied down with alien sponges.

I didn't know if I tried to disengage myself from the wires and machine if I'd accidentally shock myself. I kept yelling and finally he returned to set me free half an hour later telling me he forgot I was in the back treatment room. *Geesh*.

I could barely walk the next morning. I couldn't believe it. I went to the doctor and was sent for x-rays which showed a torn ligament in my right leg. I couldn't believe the physio had injured my leg, so to me the injury must be old, perhaps from my dive down the black ski run.

Six weeks later and lots of physio at my regular clinic I was not any better. I went on short-term disability which covered by the company where I worked. Weeks went by and I continued with physio and any other therapy that might help. I was still not getting any better and all diagnostics were negative. I was starting to doubt myself. What was going on? Sometimes you choose life, other times life chooses for you. Life is a box of chocolates and all that.

CHAPTER 10

A Medical Enigma

If you think you know it all, you are not listening.
— Marsha Johnson Evans

I was sent to a physiatrist: a doctor who specialized in rehabilitation medicine. At the end of the assessment I was advised to "make exercise my goal." I could have punched him in the head. Had he not been listening to me? I had told him I was normally very active and wasn't suffering from depression as I was well in control with my meds. I realize doctors go with what they've been taught, including somatization — the presentation of physical symptoms whose cause cannot be identified and is often thought of as depression. This truly throws a wrench in the mix for the patient. How to convince someone, anyone, that there can't be millions of people around the world with symptoms like mine — formally very active, intelligent people? Yes, I had had a whoop load of stress being a single mom and life events that knocked me for a loop, but at that point I had been managing for years and my kids were mostly self-sufficient. If any doctors believed this was a psychological condition why had all the counselling suddenly failed? Why wasn't I able to get my health back as I had always done, by starting to slowly exercise and build up my endurance? Exercise had always been my best antidepressant.

I wanted my active life back. Even though I never excelled in many sports, I loved and still love being outdoors. I especially missed swimming and hiking. I missed the feeling of peace and contentment from skiing down a beautiful mountain with white, fluffy snow and gorgeous views on a crisp sunny day. I missed hiking to a mountain meadow to a small cold lake to dip my feet in.

I did go into a depression the second summer after I got sick. I really missed all my outdoor activities. Bernie bought me a reclining tricycle and installed a battery pack on the back with a thumb lever so I could pedal a little and use the thumb lever to activate the batteries and away I would fly. We went to many parks and lakes to explore. I loved it: it gave me back a little of the outdoors I craved so much. Now that doesn't sound like a depressed woman to me. I've tried many, many times over the past twenty years to get my energy back so I can do some kind of outdoor sport. I have always been able to tell if my depression has gotten worse or if I'm having a set-back with my medical condition with a foggy brain, increased pain, horrible itching and nausea/vomiting. I was sent to an outpatient back-to-work assessment a few months after I had had to stop working. It would be held over five days at a rehab hospital. The first day I did ok. I walked around the perimeter of the hospital with the kinesiologist assessing me, and I did many other tasks that first day.

I returned the following day quite tired and sore, but I wanted to get through this assessment and get back to work.

Not even half-way through the assessment that day I fainted. I didn't feel well at all and was put in bed to rest until I didn't feel dizzy. There was a lot of concern from the medical staff. I didn't return the third day and they didn't expect me to.

My short term disability from the company I worked for was cut off unexpectedly and I had to go on the non-livable amount of money I received from employment insurance. I eventually had to cash in any savings and RRSPs. I had to get by for the several months while I waited for long-term disability.

I've listened over the years to successful people touting "Intention" — willing your bright, shiny future into existence. Just be positive and keep your eye on the goal. This is just the sort of thing I'd heard from obnoxious, privileged people. What did they think I had done so many times over the years? I believed I would be successful in my work, life and relationships; writing down goals for the month, year; making five-year and ten-year goals. Did I not believe enough? When I was a "Christian," I prayed and prayed, and could never understand why God always seemed to abandon me, leaving me hurt and bruised, without money to feed my kids. I had a job of sorts. Did that mean I failed? I couldn't keep believing in a God who could let his followers hurt. I'd had enough "lessons in life" thank you.

I was next sent to another back-to-work program, this time for overall strengthening with the goal of getting back to a nursing job and avoiding long-term disability. After two weeks of attempting to do the strengthening program laid out for me I began getting extremely exhausted and had terrible pain almost everywhere. I was getting worse and worse and nobody could tell me what was going on to make me so drastically sick. In my early thirties I had finally been diagnosed with fibromyalgia at a sports medicine clinic at the University of British Columbia, where the top doctors and physiotherapy teams often worked with the province's sports teams. During those years and years to come, many doctors dismissed diagnoses like fibromyalgia because there weren't (and still aren't) any diagnostic tests to show definitively if one has fibromyalgia unless one can get a fMRI done; but they're hard to come by and expensive.

Due to the fact that more women were diagnosed with fibromyalgia and other autoimmune conditions than men, doctors — mainly male — often believed women with fibromyalgia were actually depressed. The old somatization word again. We suckers with unexplained chronic pain and exhaustion were just a bunch of whiners looking for attention. Hardly.

Part of my second back-to-work program included an assessment by a clinical pharmacist who diagnosed me with chronic pain and put me on a whack of medication to help with the deep neuralgic pain. I wore fentanyl patches and took morphine pills for break-through pain. I was a walking pharmacy. I was finally approved for long term disability with a diagnosis of chronic pain. A middle-aged woman on enough opioids to knock over an elephant. What a life.

The multiple medications I was put on by this well-meaning clinical pharmacist initially helped a lot with the pain, but one medication — not an opioid — was way too high for me and I started exhibiting strange side effects that affected my sight and definitely my hearing. If I was around more than one person I could not understand what the person in front of me was saying. I felt like I was in a tunnel with every sound booming in my head. Truly, if I didn't know myself, I would really have thought I was descending into a hellish mental and physical breakdown. But I figured it was the meds but I was only partly correct. During any relapse I could not be around more than one person, I couldn't understand with any background noise. My brain connections seem to go hay wired and I reacted strongly to noise, lights and touch.

I changed medications but I had side-effects with it also. I continued being prescribed higher and higher doses of my fentanyl patches and I continued oral morphine.

My pain got worse no matter how many opioids (sometimes called narcotics) I took. My family practice doctor was replaced twice in three years and I just kept getting the meds prescribed, including fentanyl. I was in terrible pain a good part of the time. There were times when I lay down to sleep and my respirations seemed too low; I wasn't sure I'd make it through the night. My brain was continually in a confused state. My concentration was off. I carried on like this for at least five years. Five lost years.

I was physically weak and Bernie installed a chair lift in our three-storey house. I could barely get up a few stairs before I was winded, dizzy, and had heart palpitations. I tried another physiotherapist who suggested water rehab. I loved swimming so it sounded like a good idea. After five minutes of trying to walk in the water, the physio and lifeguard had to lift me out of the pool and made me lie down in the stretcher room until Bernie picked me up.

It certainly was frightening and there were many times I thought indeed I must be crazy. It was hard not to question myself when not one doctor really knew what was going on with me. But what could I do in that situation? I kept on "trucking" as we used to say in the 1970's. I tried many Western and Eastern therapies; some helped a wee bit at the start but eventually none worked for any length of time. Some made me markedly worse leaving me in excruciating pain crying out to God or the Universe to end my life now.

Many people with medical conditions that are not diagnosed — because the symptoms and diagnostics don't fit into the norm — tend to seek out any therapy that might provide relief. I attended one clinic upon advice of a neighbour and was appalled at the $20,000 price per year for totally unproven therapies such as oxygen rooms, diet restrictions; of course, they sold their own vitamins and supplements. I nearly lost my mind during my visit there. How could anyone not see what a bunch of crap they were selling to suffering people? I left with a bad taste in my mouth.

So, I gave up and tried to live each day the best way I could.

A few doctors encouraged me to keep up any activity that I could. I started attending a rehab pool. I loved it. I could walk slowly in the warm water for ten minutes. There was a therapy I took once a week called Watsu where a water therapist would hold me horizontal in the water and float my body through different positions and passive exercises in water. However, when I would leave the facility to drive home I began losing my way. I didn't even recognize my own neighbourhood where I had lived for over twenty years. It was like my brain was floating around and I couldn't stop it. It was terrifying.

I found I was often forgetting words or getting words mixed up like saying "cat" instead of "that." Or I would stumble to find words. My diagnosis was labelled "chronic pain" but a lot of my symptoms fit into the fibromyalgia description.

I attended a fibromyalgia meeting at the arthritis centre in Vancouver. At that time fibromyalgia did not have a "home". Patients did not fit under any medical umbrella and soon fibromyalgia was removed from the arthritis centre.

I usually don't like going to these meetings as I tend to know more about the subject than any patient I have met, and even some of the meeting leaders. It is a bad attitude of mine, perhaps, but I'm too exhausted, in too much pain, to listen to what I already know. I tend to do a lot of research on the net going to sites like Johns Hopkins, Harvard, Columbia, Stanford, and the Mayo Clinic where I read the actual research papers written and verified by doctors.

I had my walker with me; nobody else even had a cane. It was an ok meeting, mostly for meeting other people, but I was afraid I scared one lady off when she heard my story of my symptoms; she literally walked out claiming she couldn't have fibromyalgia because she was nowhere as sick as I was. I may have been in pain and exhausted beyond ridiculous, but most people would have never known if I didn't say anything. I was good at acting.

CHAPTER 11

A Few Good Men

When someone shows you who they are, believe them the first time.

— Maya Angelou

I was a very clingy girlfriend for many years, desperate to be in a relationship because if I wasn't, "something was wrong" with me. Mom always said I must keep my boyfriends in line and make them do what I wanted. WHAT? No wonder my first marriage failed.

She would push me to get and keep a man "what's the matter with you." She tormented me about my weight, which at its worst was fifteen pounds above the weight she thought it should be, which, like the old song was "A hundred and one pounds of fun, that's my little honey bun."

She even told me to go get back my so-called high school boyfriend that I had been dating all summer from the girl that "stole" him, to go to the baseball wind-up dinner and dance. Again WHAT? Why would I want to embarrass myself in front of friends to beg him to come back to me? That was ridiculous. I was angry but not enough to care. Screw him.

After I gave birth to my second child prematurely, mom and dad visited the hospital and the first thing she said to me was that I'd have to lose weight. My son was in the NICU for goodness sakes and she was telling me I was too fat again. I was actually too skinny when I got pregnant with my second son, about one hundred pounds and had only gained eighteen no matter how hard I tried to gain more. So to hear her say I needed to lose weight just dug the knife in my back a little further.

Before I met Bernie I was beginning to think I'd never meet a man who wanted to marry a single mom of three, plus two cats and a dog. I really was not good at all at picking men. I didn't see them for who they really were. These bad decisions began when I was just eighteen years old, visiting Hawaii for the first time.

I was in Waikiki with one of my school friends. I met a guy working on the catamarans on the beach at Waikiki. He looked handsome and seemed nice. He asked me out for dinner and I said yes. He asked if I liked steak or seafood, which led me to believe we were going out to a decent place.

He showed up at the door with his hair slicked back, tight jeans, and a button-down shirt — none of which were the style back then.

I didn't know what to say when I opened the door. My girlfriend, who I shared the room with, was there when he arrived. I reluctantly went with him not knowing what to expect, but he was polite and so I went. He took me to a drive-through fast food restaurant for a burger. Hmmmm, things were not looking or feeling good by that point. He insisted we go for a drive up to the Pali lookout, quite far from where we were in Waikiki. I didn't want to go; I just wanted to be back in my hotel room. But he was driving and wasn't listening to me. I was definitely wary but didn't know how to get away from him.

Up the road we went. Normally there are a few cars parked up there. It was a "lovers spot." There were no other cars when we arrived. My heart was pounding. I wanted to run but he locked the car doors. My mind was screaming, *He's going to rape me, maybe kill me!* I was terrified.

He started kissing me and I turned my head towards my door on the passenger side. He told me to quit fighting him and he had a gun in the glove compartment which he opened to show me. I sure walked right into this situation, just trying to be nice to a nerdy and scary guy.

I was a quick thinking woman — well at least when I was younger. I told him it would be nice to go for a beer, hoping we would head back to Waikiki where there were always a lot of tourists and I could get away from him.

"Great idea" he said, "but let's go to my boat, I just bought a case of beer." That wasn't the answer I wanted at all. I knew by then his intentions were to rape me. Terror hit my heart like a frozen comet. I didn't know how I was going to get out of this frightening, perhaps deadly, situation. I was eighteen years old.

As we drove towards Waikiki I asked him if we'd be alone on the boat. He wasn't sure as he shared the boat with another guy but that guy was supposed to be out for the night. His roommate was there, but I wasn't about to get into a boat with two men. That's when I said that I had a better idea, my girlfriend was going out for a bite to eat — I hoped she was back in our room by then but it was only 7:00 — and could we go to the hotel room for privacy instead? He thought that was a great idea, and so did I. If my girlfriend wasn't back, our neighbours with whom we had a joining door were always home in the early evening. I'd be safe.

But as life goes, both my girlfriend and the neighbours were out. Oh crap, what was I going to do? I had let this horrible man into my room, a clear signal that I would have sex with him. This occurred in the 1970's, well before talk of date-rape or a man's responsibility to ensure sex was mutually consented.

I told him I had to use the bathroom and I handed him a beer. I would have to get out of that room somehow. I'd stay in the bathroom with the door locked if needed.

I heard the front door open and I heard my girlfriend say hello and I let out a huge sigh. I had probably been holding my breath since we were at the Pali lookout. She plunked down on the bed closest to the bathroom where she could see me but he couldn't. I started making hand gestures to her hoping she would understand that I was trying to get him out ASAP.

Now my girlfriend was also quick-thinking. She called me over to the bed and I lay down beside her. She started talking to me like we were lovers. Now we were in our late teens and didn't know a lot about homosexuality or the fact that some men like a threesome. Thankfully he was completely turned off by our conversation and left quickly as if his butt was on fire.

I didn't see or hear about him until a year later. We asked the beach guys, where he had worked the previous year on the catamarans, if he was still around, because neither one of us wanted to see him ever again let alone go out on a catamaran with him. It turns out he had raped and beaten a woman after trying the same thing on her as he did to me. He was in jail awaiting trial. We then realized how close of a call it had been when I had gone out with him for a "steak dinner" at Jack in the Box.

I definitely felt unloved and too often tried too hard to stay in a relationship that was fun but superficial. I wanted to be loved and cherished; I had a lot of love to give but I wanted it to be reciprocal and long-lasting. I wanted and needed a lover and a friend.

After my first marriage fell apart I met a man whom I thought was "the one" but he returned to his very strict church and I wasn't able to agree with most of his religion's beliefs, even though I went to a meeting hall of his religion for a few months to hear what it was all about. I did learn a few things that made me question my dozen years of evangelical learning as an adult. But I definitely did not agree with the strong arm tactics when I told my "mentor" at this church I wouldn't be attending any longer I was told I'd be going straight to hell and was that what I wanted for my children. I ran.

Because I'm a very curious person I usually do research on the many things in life that are a puzzle to me. I read about the top religions around the world and have seen how much alike they are — except for the radicals, who turn my stomach. There is a church in my community that still does conversion therapy. That's radical and oh-so-misguided.

I loved that guy, whom I had been dating for two years, but he had to do what he had to do and I couldn't live a lie. Within the following year he married a young woman from his church, ten years younger than him, and she apparently agreed not to have children as he already had three. It was extremely hurtful. He hadn't been officially divorced when he and I dated for about a year and a half. He decided to return to his church. He had to hire a lawyer for his divorce in order to marry his sweet young thing. The lawyer hired a process server who threw a subpoena at me when I answered the door one day. I was cited as the wanton woman, the adulteress, are you KIDDING!

I was heartbroken but determined not to give up on romance. I was fed up with my choices of men I thought might make a good partner/husband. I must have been partly insane or just had bad luck. I never saw through them until I had been dating them for at least a year. There were some real winners!

One was an incredible flirt and I could never understand "what was the matter with me" that my boyfriend could be so loose with his flirtations in front of me. It was always so embarrassing. I finally got so fed up I dumped a full pint of beer on him right in front of a bunch of friends. I was applauded. Again, I loved that guy. We had so much fun cycling and skiing and partying with our friends. He wasn't keen on living with a woman with three young kids. He had already done the family route and had a daughter in her twenties. He was sixteen years older than me. Of course he ended up with a younger woman than me who had kids. We just were not meant to be a permanent couple.

Another guy, a very wealthy businessman, exercised himself to the point of having zero fat on his body. One time he came back from exercising and he smelled like ketones, a unique odour I knew from being a nurse and working with diabetics. People with uncontrolled diabetes who are about to crash will smell of ketones. It can be a very dangerous situation and if not treated the person may go into shock and die. He was also a closet alcoholic. I sure knew how to pick them!

I was treated to a view of a wealthy life by this man. Beautiful car, beautiful house, beautiful furnishings, but this was a man with serious PTSD from previous events in his life.

I had never realized how much he drank as I was usually only there on weekends.

After a very frightening trip with him abroad, I realized how mentally ill he was. Midway through our trip while we were in Crete he wanted to go for a long walk and I needed to rest. He had already been gone for a couple of hours so I made my way down to the beach. The Mediterranean Sea was so heavy with salt one could almost lay on the water and be suspended, without effort. I could have floated there all day and night. My friend walked by the beach we often went and stopped to swim with me. He seemed to be in a good mood and we swam for a while.

We went back to our room for a shower and a rest. I had a shower first. When I finished I came into the main room; he had been sleeping but woke up and began talking to me in a baby voice. I thought he was joking at first but he actually thought I was his mother. He continued talking to me like he was a little boy and continued to do so for quite awhile. It certainly freaked me out. He did not seem to be able to come back to reality. Eventually he fell back asleep. When he woke up an hour or so later he was back to normal. I was not. But I didn't confront him on the issue. What could I have said?

We went out to dinner at a nearby restaurant. He kept making ridiculous accusations about me and how I talked about my ex-husband too much. I had been divorced for more than ten years at that point. I hardly think I gave a shit about my ex-husband by then and I just shut up. I had no idea what he was on about. We still had another week on this vacation in Greece. I didn't know anybody there nor did I have my airline ticket or any money to buy another to get home and away from this terrifying situation. I had not ever seen this side of him. I was shocked but also very frightened. My blood suddenly ran cold, giving me shivers. Who was this man I had been dating for the past eighteen months?

After dinner we went back to our room nearby. He fell asleep almost instantly. It made me wonder how much he really had been drinking earlier that day or if he was taking some kind of drugs — but where would he get them? I needed some fresh air and went down to the small patio by the sea. A couple of old men were having a nightcap and they asked me if I wanted to join them. I had been sitting at a nearby table. Nobody else was sitting outdoors but it was a well-lit area just outside of the small restaurant where I could see the hotel owners and a few others having a late evening drink. I had lost my sense of trust. I was still shaking but calmed down after an evening nightcap.

Just to top the evening off there was a full moon, huge in the sky. It lay down a blanket of stars across the sea. Fishermen were out shining their lights into the water to catch squid and octopuses or octopi. Another surreal evening. So much beauty to see.

I actually felt much safer there than in my hotel room. The men I sat with had lived in this small Crete town since they were born. I nearly asked them for help to get me home but I chickened out. I was hoping it wouldn't be a critical error. I returned to our room where my friend was in a deep sleep. I crawled into the other bed and slept with one eye open all night.

The next morning it was like none of the previous day's events had happened. A lost day. I tried to put my fear out of my mind and carried on for the remaining days as if everything were fine.

We returned to Vancouver and continued to stay together on weekends. We both seemed to be drinking more when together. I didn't drink during the week, just the few years I played seasonal baseball and would go for a beer after the games.

I had another scare with him a couple of months later. I had my own health care business at the time and had a late call. My friend was expecting me to drop by afterwards and stay the night, even though it was Wednesday.

I was later than expected but had called to let him know. I arrived about 8:30 in the evening and rang the bell. He didn't come to the door so I rang again, then knocked, and then called his cell. I was just about to give up when he opened the door. He said he was already in bed reading and hadn't heard the bell.

By the time I got in bed he was acting strange. He kept talking about guns and knives. I had no idea what he was talking about. He wasn't making a lot of sense but sounded angry. I was afraid to move or speak. He didn't seem to be aware I was beside him. His tone chilled me, but he got upset when I said I should go home. "No no, don't leave me". I had the cell phone in my hand all night expecting to call 911.

He had told me when we first dated that he sometimes had nightmares. Nightmares I could handle — split personalities, guns and knives I couldn't.

We broke up.

I met my to-be-husband on an online dating site. I struck gold. Online dating was a new experience for me but I knew of a few couples who met this way and eventually got married.

Bernie (not his real name) and I dated for a couple of years while we lived in the same city. I'd spend weekends with him. He was transferred to a new job far enough away that we decided to get married. And so we did and we celebrated backwards; we first went on our honeymoon to Belize, came home and a week later had our reception on a Saturday evening, and were married the next day in the beautiful lobby of Seasons in the Park a restaurant located on top of Queen Elizabeth Park in Vancouver.

Burning Rubber

My three kids were our witnesses. After the wedding ceremony, we went into the conservatory across from the restaurant and took photos of each other in the tropical setting. It was warm and full of sounds from the colourful birds and heavenly scents from the flowering plants.

My husband was a very active guy. He could ski double black diamond runs and get down in one piece, totally unlike my acrobatic attempts. I was concerned he would get antsy missing "real" mountain biking, skiing and hiking. The first couple of years he would go up to Whistler to mountain bike while I waited at the end of the run watching biker after biker practically fly down the mountain, some with ugly looking scrapes bleeding down their limbs.

I waited patiently for my husband to get down his third or fourth run of the afternoon but he seemed to be unusually slow. I was starting to get worried but he finally limped over with his bike. He'd had a "ridiculous fall" according to him. He only cycled a few more times after that incident before giving up due to not "bouncing back" from the falls anymore.

Still, before we decided to live together and eventually get married, I made him go sit on his virtual mountain, or real mountain if he preferred, and contemplate life with me: a person often in a lot of pain and exhaustion without a proper diagnosis. A few years earlier he had done extensive travelling to New Zealand, Australia, a good part of Asia including India, Nepal, Malaysia, Thailand, and more. I didn't know if I would be able to travel again.

And so I waited for Bernie to come back from his mountain. And when he did, we got married and continued travelling. I was in a wheelchair, mind you, but my husband is a tall strong guy and easily pushed my wheelchair while carrying a large pack on his back through crowded airports.

We went to Hawaii several times, and also went to Jamaica and Mexico.

CHAPTER 12

Life Keeps Moving Forward

You never know how strong you are until being strong is your only choice.

— Bob Marley

Life carried on. Bernie worked full-time. We moved several times when he was "let go" from his previous communication tech job when that company moved south. He had applied to many places and ended up working with BC Hydro. The first five years we were transferred here and there around BC. Bernie had an apprenticeship working in Chilliwack for a year and a half and we said if a permanent position ever came up in this farming community 110 kilometres from Vancouver, we'd grab it. The people were so friendly and the pace (and traffic) was so much slower. Not so much the same nowadays.

We took various vacations, one of which was an all-inclusive vacation to Mexico. The plane had been delayed so we were a day late arriving. Then it rained for five days out of our remaining six. Somehow, we had a great time.

Our best memory was floating on the underground river through the underground caves. Now that made the trip worthwhile.

After the river experience we rented a wheelchair with the biggest wheels I'd ever seen. *Yee-ha!* Off-roading we went. Bernie was pushing me in this modified off-road wheelchair up and down the hills in this park. There wasn't a seat-belt and I figured my life as I knew it then was about to change. I didn't fall but had one hell of a great time off-roading with my husband laughing his head off and me screaming with glee. I felt alive. It had been too many years since I had had the chance to be adventurous and wild.

We made our way to the dolphin "cages". You could swim with them. I was so heart-broken seeing them in their marine cell that I could not bear getting in the water with them. I would have been delighted; I love dolphins, intelligent, happy-looking creatures. But as far as I was concerned they were in jail even though they were in the ocean. How could I contribute to this crime?

We travelled to Hawaii and stayed away from the crazy busy Waikiki. We loved to stay in Makaha with the long, powdery, white sand and turquoise water. Often we would see humpback whales frolicking in the ocean in front of us. We stayed in a small unit on the ground floor so all we had to do was open the patio door and voila — we were on the beach.

I had been going to Hawaii since I was eighteen and was not pleased at all by the "progress". Too many high-rises were blocking views. It seemed like Rodeo Drive in Waikiki and not the outdoor-oriented low-rise buildings of years past, where many open-air restaurants were located. I also loved going to the out-of-the-way bars where the locals would go to sing and dance. Progress can be good or bad but I bet the older home-grown Hawaiians were weeping. I sure was.

We travelled to Jamaica where we were treated to a brand-new, all-inclusive, amazing resort. We really were looked after well. The road to and from the airport was an eye-opener to how many Jamaicans lived in severe poverty. And here we were, living the life of luxury, with our every need met. We tipped well but maybe that was just to alleviate our own guilt.

Our lives carried on in between vacations. I took art lessons and taught myself how to knit and crochet again, something I had learned as a much younger woman. I read and researched every medical article on fibromyalgia and chronic pain; I wasn't convinced that fibromyalgia was the absolute and final diagnosis. I was far sicker than anybody I had met who said they had fibromyalgia.

One year, discussing where we should travel, my husband, Bernie suggested Thailand. I had a Thai foster girl I helped support through Plan Canada. The thought of travelling to Thailand sounded too overwhelming for me. I'd have to go in a wheelchair. How would we manage in a country where, during those years, there were not many wheel-chaired tourists? I had also heard about what I would call the nasty side of Thailand: prostitution and child prostitution. I previously overheard some men at a party who often travelled to Thailand, primarily to meet a bar girl or boy to answer to their every whim. It was cheap and turned my stomach. Why would I want to go there?

I had also heard about other very questionable activities in some of the bars. Nope and no way was I going to go to Thailand.

However, I kept thinking how nice it would be to visit my foster girl and her family in central Thailand. The deciding factor for me was a plan to go to an elephant festival in Surin, a few hours away from our foster family's small community. Ok, I was in.

CHAPTER 13

The Plan

Travel makes one modest. You see what a tiny place you occupy in the world.

— Gustav Flaubert

Bernie and I have travelled to a hot climate for a few weeks in the wintertime almost every year since we met, more than eighteen years ago

"Yes, but (I'm great with the yes-butts) what about disability access?" I could slowly walk short distances with a cane — farther with my walker — but for the distances we would cover in Thailand I would need my wheelchair. "What about the heat, what if there are stairs and no elevators, what about my medications? (at that time I was on narcotics and other meds that might not have been known or allowed in Thailand), What about...?"

Bernie replied, "We'll make do; we'll figure it out as we go along. I can always carry you over my shoulder!" He'd had to do this a few times over the years when we lived in two or three story houses.

"Yeah, not in this lifetime" I replied. Funny, very funny husband I have. Don't know what I'd do without him.

My husband is not normally a spontaneous guy, he tends to plan and research projects to the nth degree. I'm usually the one to wing it. Once I make my mind up to do something or go somewhere then all the pieces fall into place, eventually. I like to challenge myself, not to the degree I may have before my life bumped onto a different health pathway, but challenges keep life interesting.

I've had many physical and emotional upheavals in my life; I know to hang on to that rollercoaster as it catapults downward; life has a natural way of balancing itself if you let it. Thankfully there are times in our life when that rollercoaster soars upward and life is more than fulfilling — like our trip to Thailand.

I had a dream about a colourful bird, like a rainbow lorikeet, that appeared and sat on our fence. To me that was my sign that clinched my decision. I guess it didn't take much.

We planned and booked our trip to Thailand. Several legal documents from Plan Canada including a criminal record check had to be signed and sent regarding the upcoming visit of our foster girl and family in her remote village in the north-central area of Thailand. No problem. We got that done just in time.

It felt like a dream. I wasn't entirely convinced this trip was a good idea, but I couldn't back out now. Tickets were bought and plans had been made specifically for us to meet our foster girl and family. A translator and driver were hired by Plan Thailand. Train tickets were reserved. I could not back out now.

Travel day arrived. We got everything done; we were finally on our way to Thailand, a country with many challenges to vex us over the following four weeks.

CHAPTER 14

Taipei, Taiwan

I'm not the same, having seen the moon shine on the other side of the world.
— Mary Anne Radmacher

Our flight was thirteen hours to Taiwan from Vancouver, BC. We planned a two-night stopover in Taipei to get some rest before we flew the last four hours to Thailand. We travelled with Eva Air in "business class" where you could choose seats that were wider and had much more leg space and only cost a hundred or two extra between the two of us. Great for a long-legged man, like my husband, and much easier for a handicapped person. The seats also reclined partly to allow a better position for snoozing. The crew was wonderful.

After an hour of travel on a bus from the airport, we arrived at our hotel in Taipei at some ridiculous time in the early morning. It was a short walk from where the bus dropped us off to the front door of the hotel. It was obvious the architect of this hotel "neglected" to add a ramp for wheelchair accessibility. I was tired and a bit cranky from the long trip. The disabled were not usually recognized or catered to in many Asian countries at that time.

Oh crap, I thought, with more than a bit of anxiety, *How would I get up the stairs to the lobby?* I was too exhausted to make an attempt to climb on my own. I envisioned my husband flinging me up and over his shoulder, as he'd done in the past, carting me up the stairs like a sack of soggy potatoes. I wasn't happy with this scenario.

The accommodating doorman found two long pieces of wood to put on the stairs to act as a makeshift ramp. The contraption was not sturdy; every time we went up I didn't think we'd make it without dumping me onto the sidewalk. It was a steep climb. Going down was worse; all I could see was grey cement rushing toward my head, way too fast for my comfort. My wheelchair did not have a seat belt to keep me from falling forward so I held on tight, white-knuckled tight. I'm sure I looked rather interesting flying down the "ramp", holding on for dear life, hair flying in every direction, a frozen scream plastered on my face.

We repeated this scene several times over the next two days. It provided a little entertainment for the staff and people walking by. I felt humiliated in Taipei; back home in Canada there is disabled access to most buildings, restaurants, and stores. I'm somewhat shy in my wheelchair, my voice silent. People stare, drawn like a moth to a flame. They avert their eyes when mine reaches theirs. I understand it's the nature of things, curiosity about the aberrant.

Our room at our hotel was finally ready. Yay we could lie down, and lie down we did, on an unyielding futon-type mattress and hard-as-rock pillows. We slept like babies. We woke up sometime in the late afternoon feeling refreshed and hungry. In broken English, the desk clerk told us there were many places to eat around the corner on the next street.

We ventured down the recommended street in search of food. We were hungry, having missed breakfast and lunch. Breakfast on the plane had consisted of congee, somewhat similar to thick porridge, and fish. I love fish but I was already tired of fish for breakfast, fish for lunch, and fish for dinner. Not a good sign at the beginning of our Asian holiday.

We turned the corner from the hotel to the restaurant street. Hundreds of small 150cc motorbikes like Vespas or scooters were parked closely to each other, like birds on a wire, the length of the street. Motorcyclists rode side by side across the traffic lanes, zipping into the almost nonexistent spaces between cars and pedestrians.

Restaurants were located, one after another, along both sides of the street. Most of the restaurants were small with just a few plastic seats and tables inside some had no seating. The street looked like a long food court with each vendor having small, separate rooms with a glass front. It was mostly fast food, Asian style.

After walking/pushing down the side street, my stomach heaved when I saw a Taiwanese woman squatting down on the sidewalk near the gutter washing dishes in dirty water. My nausea came not so much from this woman washing her dishes in dirty water, but from the offending smell emanating from two clear bags of uncooked chicken parts — by the smell, way past their due. The open bags were sitting in the gutter inches from the woman. Black flies hovered inside the bags slamming into each other, wrestlers in a ring, fighting for a taste of the rotten meat. In a wheelchair one is closer to the street, sidewalk, and sewers; everything stinks.

I turned my head and shouted, "Hon, push faster, please!" (Canadians are so polite). I felt like swearing a blue streak and vomiting at the same time.

We carried on and found a mini restaurant that looked and smelled clean. All the menu signs were in Taiwanese and very few people spoke English. Fortunately, most restaurants displayed their food as hard plastic molds in the shapes and colours of each food item plus what comes with each order. The food was excellent. Our imminent starvation was thwarted for the time being. It all stayed in our tummies too.

CHAPTER 15

Ascension

There are no foreign lands. It is the traveller only who is foreign.

— Robert Louis Stevenson

The next day, feeling less sleepy, we toured around the city using Taipei's rapid transit system (MRT), similar to Vancouver's sky train or the subways located in most large cities. Bernie seemed to know where he was going so I went along for the ride, so to speak. We headed to a gondola near the zoo, for a ride up to a temple and tea houses.

We managed to disembark at the correct station at the Taipei zoo. There was one tourist waiting in line at the zoo but we were going to the Maokong Gondola which was much busier; we couldn't see the start of the line and there must have been thirty to forty people waiting for a ride up the four kilometre hill leading to the temple.

On the walk from the MRT station to the Maokong Gondola, it started raining lightly. It started pouring as we reached the end of the line of the now water-logged tourists. The temperature had dropped. All of us were shivering; thank goodness the line was moving fast. I had on a yellow plastic rain cover that we purchased from an enterprising Taiwanese woman waiting at the end of the gondola line selling rain covers to most of the approaching customers for about two dollars Canadian. She made a bundle that day.

Living in the rainforest, as we do back home in Vancouver, we are used to the rain. We don't like it but if you want to get anything done outside from the month of October to the end of May, then you'll likely do it in the rain.

We shuffled along at a decent rate. As we approached the entrance, we could see each gondola open its doors, devouring groups of rain-drenched tourists. We watched them disappear slowly into the clouds up the steep four kilometre hill to a Buddhist temple and several tea houses. Finally it was our turn on the gondola for a cool, misty ride uphill, slowly enshrouded by clouds. Kind of like my life then, I felt I was disappearing into mist, my former self wiped away.

I'm sure the view is usually spectacular, but it wasn't that day. The largest building, at the top of the gondola, is the Sanxuan Temple which we explored with the many other curious tourists. We took a walk down the road where several tea houses were located on both sides of the street. We were still shivering in the rain so we searched for a tea house without too many stairs for me to climb. We found one to sit in and rest and drink some hot tea. By the time we finished our delicious delicate tea it had stopped raining and the sun was breaking through the clouds.

On our way back to the hotel via the MRT we managed to get a little lost. Looking confused, we scoured the Taiwanese signs above our heads at the midway station. Walkways to several different lines of the MRT went five different ways to five different trains. A man in an electric wheelchair approached and offered his assistance. Simon was Taiwanese and spoke very good English. I'll never forget this man; he talked up a storm and was so excited to be practicing his English with people from Canada. He declared his love of hockey and even knew teams and player names. Bernie and I are true hockey fans; we were surprised to hear good English and talk of hockey from a Taiwanese guy in a wheelchair half-way around the world. It was surreal. We followed him from one train to the next using elevators here and there. We never would have found our way back to the hotel if it weren't for Simon.

Back to the hotel for another rest. There was a minor — no a major — panic attack before we left for dinner; I couldn't find my medications. I found my blister packs that held the majority of my medication, but where were the bottled medications like 180 capsules of morphine and the fentanyl patches? "Bernie, help me look, I can't find the rest of my meds." We searched every bag twice and emptied out all the drawers. Bernie picked up the phone to call the desk when he spotted a small black bag under the wheelchair. I hadn't a clue how it got there but all meds were accounted for. Phew! I wasn't keen on going cold turkey in a foreign country.

The people in Taiwan were friendly, helpful, polite, and patient in crowded spaces. No one was pushing and shoving to get onto or off the train. We were astonished to see people lining up, one person behind the other, on the platform of the train. There was even a handicapped entrance to the train. Not one person tried to budge their way past us: this has happened often enough in almost every other country we have visited. It's always refreshing touring a clean city where millions of people are polite and tolerant.

The next morning we prepared for the three and a half hour flight to Bangkok, Thailand.

CHAPTER 16

Bangkok

I Can Taste the Air and See the Heat
— *KLI*

We arrived in Bangkok at 11:45 AM. The ride in a taxi from the airport, Suvarnabhumi, was unsettling. The air was stifling hot; we were covered in sweat instantaneously after leaving the air-conditioned airport to find a taxi. The traffic was more frenetic than anywhere else I'd travelled, well except for Rome, whose traffic was a similar state of insanity. Often the first sight I saw in a developing country, just outside of the airport, was the pre-urban area, marked by crowding, dirty run-down housing, abject poverty, and social disorganization. It's almost a given in many countries. Think India.

The hotels and apartments were huge, very tall and wide, and built close to each other. There is no room to breathe in Bangkok.

Before we arrived in Thailand, I had a different picture in mind of what Bangkok would look like. I was very wrong.

When I took a dying patient to Myanmar in 1999, I flew into Yangon airport. As I flew over the countryside, I didn't see any cities; mostly I saw empty countryside, people riding bikes on rust coloured roads and lots of lush, dark green vegetation. I only saw one car spewing red dust in every direction. I saw small villages scattered here and there. I pictured Thailand being similar to Myanmar; I was way off.

Bangkok is huge (the population is over 11 million and swells to more than 15 million during the day with tourists and workers). My image of Thailand vaporized when reality struck. I was overwhelmed by the noxious, crowded city.

Bangkok is a polluted dirty city and definitely not wheelchair-friendly. The only entrance to the hotel we could use had a ramp in a side alley where trucks delivered to the many hotels. The alley stunk to high heaven. There was a large sewer drain, covered but with several holes which allowed putrid odours to escape. Unfortunately, I was stuck close to the sewer while Bernie went into the hotel to book us in. I was so mad. I was exhausted, thirsty, and stuck in my wheelchair with the large backpack beside me and other smaller travel bags on my lap. In his haste to get us booked in, Bernie hadn't realized how close I was to that stinking sewer. This was not fun at all. I was getting crankier by the minute.

Bernie managed to book a suite online at this beautiful hotel for a great introductory price; in other words what we could afford. The suite was huge and suited us just fine. By the time we unpacked, the harsh day had receded into the gloaming hour — except it didn't look gloaming to me, more like the witching hour for murderers and thieves.

We finally got settled into our beautiful room. Phew. We had lots of room and a large bathroom. There were floor-to-ceiling windows allowing us a wide view of the city of Bangkok.

Bernie asked if I would like to go outside to find a place to eat. "No, I don't want to go out," I said. "I'm really tired and need to rest." I was tired, but that was not the reason I refused to go. I was terrified to go out there in my wheelchair. My usual bravado slipped out the door following Bernie.

I peeked out the window and looked at the street a block away. There were no cars on this street after 7:00 PM; a night market completely covered the street and sidewalks. The vendors were crushed side by side over two square blocks with a narrow path between. White awnings covered the many kiosks appeared like huge, gleaming, white canvases waiting for Jackson Pollock.

There must have been a million people (well, maybe that's an exaggeration) crammed together buying or selling. I tried not to look, but I was drawn to the window like a curious cat. The sight overwhelmed me. *I want to go back home. I really can't do this, I'm not that brave.* I laid on the king size bed, feeling small — very small — and quickly fell into an unsettled slumber.

Twenty minutes later I stood up and went back to the hotel window, hands over my eyes, trying very hard to calm myself. I dropped my hands from my face; the scene was spectacular, like going for a drive on Christmas Eve after a fresh snowfall. Millions and millions of lights blinking throughout the city turned the cacophony of daytime into a luminescent symphony of light.

Will this city turn back, like Cinderella after midnight, to its usual daytime lugubrious self? I hated to sound like a pessimistic Eeyore but the answer was "More than likely." For now, I felt calm gazing out the window at sparkling jewels against the blackness of night.

I heard a knock at the door, probably someone with our dinner. Whatever it was it got my stomach growling in anticipation. Bernie was very excited to be back in Thailand and he spoke about the streets as if there were no issue at all. He is six feet tall after all and could see over most people's heads.

I get upset and a little claustrophobic when I'm in a wheelchair among a crowd of people where all I can see are bellies, butts, and boobs. Back home, if I need to do some personal shopping Bernie often takes me in the chair. For instance, a few weeks before our trip, I went to buy some good sandals.

I asked the saleswoman a few questions regarding the sandals and at every question I asked she gave the answer to Bernie, my six-foot-tall husband. Not once did she attempt to look me in the eye and answer my questions.

This happens too often back home. It infuriates me to the bone. Even in this day and age — at least in North America — some people are still uncomfortable around people who are different and don't know how to act or react when confronted by a person with disabilities. Is it fear or just human angst?

Bernie and I went to bed early and had an exceptional slumber for ten hours. I felt much better the next morning. I looked out the window with eyes wide open. The scene had changed again. In broad daylight, after a good nights' sleep and the night market gone, I could see actual streets: people walking on the sidewalks and plenty of cars, trucks, mopeds, tuk-tuks, and crazy taxi drivers.

There was a ton of traffic, constantly honking and squeezing into minute spaces between vehicles big and small to get to other lanes, four or five away. Drivers must close their eyes and send prayers to Buddha for a safe journey. It seemed to work, we didn't see or hear any traffic accidents while we were there but I later learned there were hundreds every day. It is a large city.

A brand new day, *I'll be alright,* I said to myself. *Be brave.*

Looking out the window I could clearly see the river, as well as one of the king's palaces across the street from our hotel. It was huge and opulent, spreading over a few blocks of prime real estate. This palace reminded me of the one in the movie *The King and I*. The present king would be turning eighty in early December. Bangkok was decorated in his honour.

Later, I would learn a lot of Thai people would get rid of the monarchy. These discussions occurred behind closed doors; it could be disastrous if the wrong people overheard the conversation. We had to choose clothes to wear that were neither red nor yellow. It was too difficult keeping straight the correct colour for the correct political party so we avoided wearing dreaded yellow or red. Even though we were farand (foreigners) we didn't want to offend anyone.

Asian culture is all about saving face; yours or someone else's. We were visitors surrounded by a different culture than ours. We changed some of our behaviour to reflect Thai culture. In Bangkok and in temples or palaces all over Thailand, women must cover their shoulders and wear skirts or pants that cover their knees. Public displays of affection are frowned upon, same with swearing. Not a good way to endear oneself to the Thai people.

When Bernie and I were discovering Bangkok we would see a few visitors walking around the city in beach clothes; not a problem back home or in the southern regions of Thailand near the beaches, but not appropriate attire for the rest of Thailand and never in temples or in any of the king's palaces.. I didn't learn enough about Bangkok before we arrived but at least I read up on do's and don'ts while in Thailand. We also took private Thai language lessons before our first trip which helped immensely during our travels.

We ate a scrumptious breakfast on the sixtieth floor of the hotel overlooking the city, which seemed far less scary than the night before.

I was still apprehensive going out of the hotel for some sightseeing, but I didn't want to get stuck alone in the room waiting while Bernie explored the city. I swallowed the lump in my throat, got on the wheelchair, and away we went out the back entrance then down the steep ramp that led to the odiferous alley —the front entrance had stairs. We turned the corner onto a busier street and I was immediately swallowed up by people selling their wares at make-shift kiosks side by side. I groaned: I had thought all the sidewalk vendors were only out in the evening.

Customers filled the sidewalks like water in a jar of sand; every minute spot on the sidewalk was stuffed with people and vendors. I'm five feet tall and weigh 100 pounds soaking wet, not a large person. Before accidents changed my life I was always uncomfortable in a crowd. I became invisible to others; in the wheelchair it was much worse. This was what I'd been dreading ever since we arrived.

Thank goodness Thailand had traffic cops on corners of busy streets. We waited until the policeman saw us and he quickly whistled the cars to stop. *OK no problem, we have plenty of time to race across the street.* Yeah, we made it. Bernie sort of knew where he was going; after all it had been a few years since he was last in Thailand.

A few blocks later we stopped at the most intimidating intersection of any we saw on this trip. We arrived at an intersection where double or triple traffic lanes met at a six-cornered stop. The intersection looked like an octopus with tentacles stretching out in six directions. We waited for the light and the traffic cop signalled for us to cross to the other side. Bernie pushed the wheelchair as fast as he could, but not once in our two trips to Thailand did we make it across this particular intersection before cars and vespas charged toward us like angry hornets. Every single time we crossed this insane road I put my hands over my eyes. If we were going to die, I didn't want to watch.

Often we didn't make it all the way across the street without having to stop half-way. Once we had to stop on a very narrow island where construction was going on. We never saw any workers, just an inconvenient block to our safe passage. Yellow construction tape barricaded the only part of the treed island we could stand on. So big, tall Bernie and me in a wheelchair had to stop on the road trying to be small, and we squeezed as close to the small island as possible. I, of course, had my eyes closed. I could feel disaster breathing down my neck.

I had to get out of my wheelchair and walk over a tree stump, then sit again in my wheelchair, which was still on the street. I was terrified, stuck in the middle of the maniacal traffic charging at us from six corners. I covered my eyes again; I was sure one of the cars would clip us.

What a terrible job it must be for a traffic cop; they all wear face or gas masks but the pollution from the heavy traffic must permeate the body. There is no such thing as emission control in Thailand. The temperature that day was a muggy 38 degrees Celsius. So hot at times we could smell burning rubber, which happened to be my wheelchair tires; we carried no spares. They were down to the metal by the time we got home.

We found a taxi after we crossed the street. We could breathe a little easier in the taxi —at least in that one. As we drove around the city we noticed the many gold and white monuments honouring the king. Workers were scrubbing and polishing temples, the palaces, and every ornate white and gold sculpture around the city. The king, his wife, and son (king-to-be), lived in opulence.

We saw many temples all over Bangkok and in every town and city we visited. Most of them were very colourful with a lot of shining gold paint and gold flakes. There were many styles of temples, from a simple wooden one built on water, to one made entirely from bottles — all kinds of old fashioned pop and beer bottles. Truly amazing to construct a "full service" temple made from glass bottles.

We asked our taxi driver to let us off near the water-taxi stand. There were six stairs to negotiate. I always brought my cane for times like this.

I struggled to get down the stairs; Bernie carried the wheelchair down the steps to the crowded water taxi which was similar to a large, partly covered gondola with several wooden benches.

A woman in the water taxi helped me into the boat. Bernie got the wheelchair on board but still had one foot on the ledge of the boat and the other on the pier. The boat was rocking; the driver started to go forward, with Bernie dangling precariously over the water, one foot still on the pier. He was about to fall in the water or keep doing the splits until he separated like a wishbone from a turkey carcass.

People were shouting at the driver to stop, which he did eventually; Bernie came dangerously close to falling into the river, but he somehow made it in the boat. Phew.

The river was so polluted I didn't want Bernie or me to fall in that toxic mess; there would be nothing left of us except maybe skeletons. Now that we were in the boat, as opposed to outside the boat, we could relax a little. My heart was still pounding as the driver gunned the boat, moving rapidly up the river to the next stop where we were headed.

On either side of the river people lived in squalor: a shanty town built on the river banks. This was not the paradise I had imagined, and although I was well aware of the deep-seated poverty pervasive in every developing country, this was beyond belief.

Apartments, if you could call them apartments, were side by side and two to three stories high. Box-housing. Children played in the only place they could, on the banks of the repugnant river. Laundry hung from many of the apartments, some were advertising laundry service. Televisions were loud; to me, thinking as a North American, it was bizarre, looking at some of the poorest people living in shabby dwellings where ninety percent of them had TV's. I didn't know how they afford a TV. They must have been dirt cheap there.

It was difficult for me to assimilate and accept the massive discrepancy between the rich and poor of Thailand: not just Thailand, but many other developing countries.

The incongruence was startling. The King and the Masses. The poor were so very, very poor.

Bernie and I were blue collar workers, although I'm retired now from my job as a registered nurse. We weren't "rolling in the dough" but lived a modest and very happy life in the country. In Thailand we could have lived as royalty if we wanted, but we didn't.

After our hairy ride on the boat we headed for the train station to confirm our tickets to travel northeast to the town of Surin (population 46,673) then onward to the town of Sisaket (population 46,000), close to where our foster girl and family lived. Surin and Sisaket are also the names of two of the mid-northeastern provinces in Thailand.

It was a good thing we checked our train reservations; it took quite a while for the stationmaster to find our names in the archaic system.

After confirming our tickets for the six-hour overnight train from Bangkok we headed to the infamous tourist area on Khaosan Road to have lunch, shop for T-shirts, and take in the atmosphere. Many back-packers stay near Khaosan Road; lodgings are inexpensive and the food in the restaurants is out-of-this-world delicious. Khaosan Road is blocked off to cars.

There were travellers from every part of the world packed into the small stores. It was much too difficult to push my wheelchair around in the discommodious teeny-tiny stores. I was able to walk inside a few using my cane. I was a little nervous leaving my wheelchair outside on the crowded sidewalk; however, it was always in the same spot we had left it. It is not common for Thai people to steal; I was more worried about the tourists. Nobody was interested in my soft, partly melted, large-wheeled chair.

We had lunch in one of the outdoor restaurants. It was the best lunch we'd had in a week. We chose coconut soup full of veggies and three different kinds of mushrooms as well as sweet-and-sour prawn. The taste of everything was delectable; almost too heavenly to describe. I never expected the food to be this good. My mouth is watering just remembering. Unfortunately, we forgot the name of the place and couldn't remember where on the street it was located when we returned the following year.

I managed to buy some souvenirs and t-shirts. Bernie bought his usual, coveted Rin Tin Tin and Calvin & Hobbes t-shirts. After we were shopped out, we headed back to the hotel in a (land) taxi; we decided to stay on terra firma while in Bangkok at least. We had a massage in the hotel spa. Ummm, very relaxing; this was followed by a delicious dinner at the hotel restaurant tand then back to our room to read and soon after, a refreshing sleep.

CHAPTER 17

Shopping Around

I have a love-hate relationship with shopping; I hate going but I love new things

— *K.I.*

We ventured out again for more shopping. We wanted to get as much done as we could so we could leave our large backpack at the hotel baggage room while we were up north.

I was getting much less freaked out when we ventured outside. I still closed my eyes when we crossed certain streets. Bernie took me to a five-story shopping mall not too far from our hotel. It had an elevator. We did "shop 'till we dropped." There was no way I was going to be able to try on clothes, I was already fatigued. My daughter is a little smaller than me, weight-wise. She's a whole 2" taller than me so I usually buy the same size as myself. I couldn't find much for the boys.

We left the store after an afternoon of shopping and returned to our hotel room to try on the garments. Not one fit; now we had to go back to the same stores by the next day or we couldn't exchange them. The size of clothing did not follow American apparel. It was in a league of its own.

CHAPTER 18

A day from Hell

I'll have a Cafe-Mocha-Vodka-Valium Latte to go please.

— Unknown

The day started out ok. We had a good breakfast then went for another massage in the hotel spa. I was looking forward to our day; it was going to be a long one. We were leaving on the overnight train to Surin at 8:40 PM. I was going to have another relaxing massage before our six-hour journey by train.

I chose to have a Thai massage. I was amazed I had any workable body parts after the masseuse finished with me. I asked her for a medium-pressure massage, not knowing she didn't speak a word of English. I managed to hold onto my screams until she was finished. I had heard Thai massages were painful; something I should have stayed away from considering that part of my physical problem was chronic pain.

Later, I was surprised at how much better my muscles felt and my headache was gone, but my elbow felt broken. The masseuse did a lot of stretching and some spinal manipulation. My elbow had been stretched too far, one way or another and I couldn't apply even light pressure to my arm. Over the next week the elbow pain settled, then disappeared unless the elbow got bumped — then I was right back in pain. It was like having a constant knock on my (non) funny bone.

We returned to our room for a breather before we headed out again. As I was resting Bernie popped out to buy three new dress shirts at one of the sidewalk kiosks close to the hotel. They even fit. Hard to buy clothing for a 6' tall man with long arms in most Asian countries.

We packed and repacked the very large backpack to leave at the hotel while we were travelling north and take a smaller more manageable one. Would you believe it, we had more shopping to do. We only had one day to return the clothes that didn't fit for my daughter and me. Bernie didn't manage to buy any clothing at this six-story department store, but he found some cheap CDs; he was happy with his purchases.

After exchanging the clothes we took a taxi to Khaosan Road for one more shot at shopping in stores for tourists. We didn't buy much. Afterwards, we headed to an alley behind Khaosan Road to have a late lunch at the world-famous vegetarian restaurant; Mai Kaidee. Delicious. I took several photos of scrappy alley dogs and interesting (tongue-in-cheek) people roaming up and down the alley. It was better than watching TV.

If you wanted to cook Thai food this is the place to be; cooking lessons were on-going. We wished we had the time to take a lesson or two. Bernie was a great cook, but we were headed out of Bangkok for a week. Maybe there would be time when we returned to Bangkok from our northern adventures.

By the time we finished our "lunch" it was already after 5:00; we needed to get back to the hotel to pick up the less-large back-pack we needed for the next leg of our journey.

It took some time to hail a cab that would actually slow down; drivers came close but when they realized I was in a wheelchair they took off. Finally one pulled close and actually stopped; we got in and the taxi moved three feet forward then stopped again.

We were in a traffic jam, maybe there had been an accident or maybe this was normal dinner-time traffic flow. Our driver spoke some English and kept apologizing for the jammed traffic. We were patient for a while. Start and stop was all we were doing and not getting anywhere fast or even slowly. We realized we must find another way to get back to the hotel soon or we would miss our train that night, which would mean we would miss the elephant festival and possibly meeting our foster girl.

We paid the taxi driver for our fifty-seven *baht* (Thai currency) trip, equal to $1.70 US plus a good tip, then jumped out of the taxi and headed out on our own. Thankfully, Bernie knew the way back to the hotel. I was sitting in my wheelchair laden down with shopping and the camera bag. Bernie had the rest of our purchases hanging from each arm.

My long-legged husband accelerated his walking/jogging and pushed me in the wheelchair at break-neck speed. Not once had we seen anybody else in a wheelchair in Thailand, tourists included, so we were a curious looking couple. Later, during one of our Bangkok stops between visiting other parts of the country, we saw a man with most of both legs amputated. I recalled a book I had read; Rohinton Mistry's *A Fine Balance* where one of the characters describes a beggar he sees "slumped upon a small wooden platform fitted with castors which raised him four inches off the ground." The man in front of us was in a similar contraption; a boy was pulling him by a rope tied to the platform.

Bernie was still running and pushing me at a rapid pace. My face was frozen in a scream like Edvard Munch's painting.

We headed for the dreaded water-taxi; we didn't have any choice but to take it one more time. It was the most direct way back to the hotel. It would take another twenty to thirty minutes to go around on foot and we were running out of time. The ride on the water-taxi was less stressful than the first time, but not by much. After the boat ride and a climb up some stairs, I was back in my wheelchair. Bernie was going as fast as he was able; we still had four long blocks to our hotel. It was getting late, well after 7:00 PM. The train was leaving in an hour and a half.

The ubiquitous street vendors were all around us. We were squeezed out onto the street by a few people taking too much room on the sidewalk. Finally, drenched in sweat, we made it to our hotel room for a quick wash-up and grabbed the bags we needed for Surin. The train was to leave at 8:40 and we were told to get to the station thirty minutes prior to departure. It was now 8:00 PM.

The hotel doorman whistled for a taxi, shoved the wheelchair into the trunk, and stuffed the backpack beside me in the back seat. We hit another traffic hold-up; our wonderful taxi driver asked us if he could take the freeway to get to the train on time. He was concerned we might not want to pay the extra *baht*, equal to two or three American dollars. "Yes!" we both implored.

At this point I'm sure we would have paid 100 dollars to get to the station on time. We tipped our driver well; not much money to us but a days' worth of cab fares for him. We had five minutes before the train was due to leave; thanks to good forward thinking on Bernie's part to have picked up the tickets earlier that day, we headed directly to the number eight platform. The sun had already set; we glanced at the silver train.

Something was wrong; this train had two wheel brakes entirely off and in several pieces lying on the ground near the train. The brakes needed to be changed apparently. "What, you've got to be kidding me? " I said to Bernie. This situation did nothing to instill confidence in either one of us. I took a deep breath and sighed while Bernie spoke to one of the station crew men. Time is a totally different concept in Thailand especially for scheduled events like train and bus time schedules.

For fifteen minutes we diligently watched the crew work on the brakes and wheels — not that we knew how to fix trains, it just helped to reassure us a wee bit that all the parts were back together. They weren't; we were a little concerned. Oh well, we climbed on board anyway and found our first-class sleeper cabin. First class is comparable to third class in other countries. Our cabin was small, much smaller than I had imagined, a virtual closet. As we went along this trip, we encountered many unusual experiences and practices; I've learned to always expect the unexpected because that's often the way life goes.

Bernie, at six feet and 200 pounds, took up a good part of the cabin. There was a futon style sofa/sleeper with just enough room for us to sit side-by-side, and a really small sink, a "Barbie" sink with a mirror above. The purser stopped by to make up our beds; the upper bunk was pulled down and the bottom of the futon laid flat. He offered us a small menu to order something to eat and drink. We had missed having dinner due to our arduous day. We were thankful for whatever was available.

After our snack I needed to go to the bathroom. Bernie helped me walk past four cabins to the bathroom location. I stepped in and closed the door. "Oh, no!" I cried as I realized this was one of the many floor toilets we would need to use in Thailand. It looked like an individual shower stall with a drain in the middle of the floor. There was a one inch ledge to prevent fluids from spilling over and running out the door, and a hose, for cleaning oneself, attached to the far wall, about six inches from the ground. I've had to use toilets like this on other trips when I was able-bodied — try using this type of toilet on a rumbling, jerking train. I couldn't lift my right leg off the floor at the best of times, and I lose my balance easily. Needless to say things didn't work out and I had to wash my clothes (as well as my runners) in the tiny cabin sink. Humiliating experience. Thank goodness my husband loves me so much; he didn't even bat an eye when I returned to the cabin. He got off the upper bunk to help me. What a guy.

We lay on our bunks and read for a while. As soon as laid his head on the pillow he started snoring — he was happy getting well-deserved sleep. I was beginning to love the sound of the train on its tracks as it thundered forward into the night. It was dark and I could no longer see out of the window. I read for another hour then fell asleep, lulled by the sound and motion of the train.

CHAPTER 19

Surin

What doesn't kill me makes me stronger.
— Albert Camus

We arrived in Surin at 5:00 AM, only a half hour late, which was extremely good, apparently according to the Thais. We took a motorized tuk-tuk or rickshaw to our hotel in Surin just a few blocks away, too far to walk. There were hardly any people around other than Thais: the hotel was quiet. Life in any town is somewhat peaceful at 5:00 AM.

I was once again amazed at the size of Surin; about 46,000 Thais. One spoke English.

Our room was very comfortable; we slept until 11:00 AM, had a shower, then ventured out of the hotel for more surprises. There were elephants everywhere and I mean everywhere. What an incredible sight to see. My daughter and I loved elephants; I was in awe of the majestic beasts. I heard one trumpeting down the small road from the hotel to the main street. Bernie and I headed in that direction and soon found the animal that matched the noise. I had never been this close to an elephant in my life. I was awestruck by the elephants' gentleness and bigness.

The Surin Elephant Festival (or Surin Elephant Roundup, as it is also called) occurs annually on the third Saturday in November. The usual soporific town quadruples with pilgrims arriving from every country for the weekend (Friday and Saturday). Some arrive by car, others by train, bus, tuk-tuks, small motorcycles, and on elephants. The elephant is held with great esteem by the Thai people, even though many elephants — from a North American point of view — are overworked and not treated with dignity.

Many of the festival participants, including elephants, come from Thai Klong, a village about forty kilometres north of Surin. The festival began in the 1960s and has grown so large the few hotels in Surin cannot cope with the onslaught of visitors and many need to find accommodations in nearby towns.

We explored a good part of Surin that afternoon. We wanted to purchase some small gifts for the foster family we would see the next day. In broken Thai and English, we managed to communicate what items we were looking for to a few vendors. It's amazing how often pantomime works.

We kept going, not knowing where exactly, but we liked adventures. We knew enough Thai to ask for directions to the hotel if needed. We walked all over town; Bernie sure got his exercise that day. In this part of the country (Sisaket and Ubon Ratchathani) the weather is very hot and dry. The average temperature from November to the end of February is 32 degrees Celsius; April and May are the hottest, with an average temperature of 36 degrees Celsius. The temperature varies depending upon the location in Thailand. In the central-north the land is dry: Bangkok is more humid, and the further south you travel the humidity increases. Near the mountainous regions the temperature can plummet at night to 2 degrees Celsius.

We followed the signs to the stadium where the elephant festival would be held. We came to a street that looped around a long canal. Along both sides of the canal were long tables with all kinds of fruit packed together tightly. There were tons of pineapple, bananas, and mangoes: almost all tropical fruits one could think of. It was for the elephants' parade and breakfast the next morning. Too bad we had to miss it; we would have to leave the hotel in Surin early in the morning to catch a train to Sisaket and onward to the train station closest to the village where our foster girl and family lived. *Oh well, you can't do everything,* although I try.

By the time we got back to the hotel, not only were there more elephants "parked" on the streets, tied to posts like horses in old western movies, there were significantly more people —and we had thought we had the town to ourselves. Wow, where did all the people come from? We weren't gone that long, it seemed. We could barely move in the hotel lobby. There were so many people; tourists like us were in Surin for the elephant festival. We chatted with a few newcomers and learned that some attended the elephant festival every year; one gent had been coming back every year for the past thirty. I could understand the attraction. I wouldn't have minded coming back at least one more time.

We had another shower and snooze before we headed out for dinner at The Thai restaurant (that's the actual name). The food was unbelievably delicious. I was definitely hooked on Thai.

On our way out, we walked down the pedestrian road from the hotel to the street. There was a beer garden, tourists wandering about, and a few elephants. The trainers were letting tourists feed the elephants. I was in heaven. One of them wrapped his trunk around me, probably looking for more food, but the hug was mind-blowing. I had never been that close to an elephant before.

We continued on to the road and passed by several elephants parked side by side with their backs facing the road. One of the trainers, or *mahout*, was trying to get his elephant to move backwards. It was sort of like backing up a car. The elephant refused to budge and trumped loudly a few times as his master tugged his rope harder. The *mahout* didn't see us, me in my wheelchair and Bernie trying to push me around the crowds of people and elephants. The elephant backed out without a problem after we had passed by. They are huge pachyderms; backing up onto us was not what the elephant wanted, nor did we; it would not be a good way to end our trip. Squashed by elephant — unusual death report.

It seemed as if the elephant sensed us, or our bit of panic, and waited to back up when we were well out of the way. Nice, considerate elephant. Phew.

We arrived at the restaurant and ordered a large beer, not quite sure what they meant by large. The beer bottle must have been at least a litre and half; we easily managed to have four tall glasses between us. In Surin when you want to order a beer, a glass of wine, or bottled water in a restaurant you receive the whole large bottle. Good to know. We nearly ordered two large beers, thinking it would be like ordering a pint of beer in a bar back home. Oh well, we weren't driving.

By the time we finished our dinner I was in a terrible amount of pain even after drinking the beer, so we headed back to the hotel. I took some medication but this type of deep body pain transcended any medication; the only way through that misery was to ride the pain, a reluctant war horse. I tried not to think about the journey to see our foster girl tomorrow. We had had a few punishing days of craziness and it had caught up. I went to bed and had a nice long sleep.

CHAPTER 20

The Big Day

Avoiding danger is no safer in the long run than outright exposure. Life is either a daring adventure or nothing.

— Helen Keller

Bright and early the next morning we had breakfast in the hotel restaurant, among hundreds of other guests, and then waited for the hotel shuttle to drive us to the train station for our visit with our foster girl. Our train was due to leave at 8:30 AM. We ordered the shuttle van for 8:00 AM to take us the five minute ride to the train station. Bernie and I were beginning to get a little nervous the longer we waited for our ride — this was our big day. This was the main reason we came to Thailand, to have the privilege to meet our foster girl and family.

The shuttle van finally arrived at 8:15. "That's alright; we'll still make it on time."

On any other day this would be true; today the coalition of tourists made negotiation of streets and sidewalks impossible. It was the morning of the parade which took the elephants around the city to their morning buffet along the canal. The festival was being held in a stadium located in an opposite direction from the train station. It didn't matter: cars, trucks, vespas, tuk-tuks, and people were absolutely everywhere. Our driver knew we had a train to catch at 8:30; he was unsure which direction to drive through the hordes of people and vehicles to get us to the station on time. He turned abruptly and took a short-cut, attempting to maneuver the van through alleys with crater-sized potholes. The taxi's suspension (or lack of), pummelled our bodies up, down, and sideways. I was in a lot of pain; our situation deteriorated. The driver didn't speak one word of English, except "ok". I thought he was asking us if he should go this way, or that; ok? Well, heck, we didn't know, we were all turned around. We should have walked.

The driver turned left onto a narrow one-way street. Oh boy, it was definitely not the best choice; all roads were traffic-jammed. That particular road, being a one-way street, was especially bad. There was nowhere to turn the vehicle around. In the meantime, we got stuck behind two large trucks and more cars came behind us with the same thought as our driver. Intelligent people on vespas flew past us on both sides. I felt like sticking my tongue out at them, but that just didn't seem appropriate at the moment … well ya, it did but...

It was now 8:25 and Bernie and I were starting to get very, very concerned — as opposed to the merely very concerned we had felt ten minutes ago. We saw a traffic cop at the head of our street; we were still not moving, what the heck was going on? Bernie jumped out of the shuttle van and headed to the main intersection where the cop was supposed to be directing all four directions of the traffic. The truck at the top of this narrow side street intersection, two or three vehicles ahead of us, had not moved for five minutes.

Bernie asked the cop, nicely, in Thai, to let some of the trucks and cars get onto the main drag where we and others needed to be. Bernie returned to the car and finally the cop signalled our lane of traffic to go ahead. He let one and only one truck through the intersection. *Aaaaagh!*

It was now 8:30: train departure time. Bernie went up to the traffic cop again and explained we needed to catch a train five minutes ago. The cop, kindly (ha-ha) allowed our lane to move. Again he only let one truck turn. It was 8:35. What were we going to do? We discussed taking a bus to the train station where we were to meet our translator and driver. We didn't know the bus schedule and decided it was probably too far for us to walk from where we were. We might as well stay in the car. What a disaster. We inched our way to the main intersection; and we almost pumped our hands in the air, but restrained ourselves. We needed to turn left toward the train station but the cop only allowed us to turn right, which was just as packed with vehicles as all the other streets we had been. Bernie and I looked at each other, shook our heads in dismay, and realized we'd missed the train. Now we had no choice but to try to get to the bus station and call our translator and driver to let them know when where we would be if we could make it at all. We were so disappointed; the day's arrangements had been based on the availability of the driver and translator, as well as the family of our foster girl, who were not able to visit us on any other day but that day.

Suddenly our driver made a turn into an alley with even deeper potholes unbelievably worse than the other streets or alleys. Where was he going now? It appeared the driver was headed back to our hotel; but we needed to get to the bus station. We tried to explain to him to take us to the bus station instead and he replied, "Ok.»

Now he was driving across a field, also full of potholes. I was incredulous as my pain started to rise. We were in the field behind the train station, which was good except we needed to get down a three foot drop, then scurry across several sets of old train tracks, thick wires of some kind, and two gullies to the platform of the train which was three feet up. It was 8:40, our train was overdue, which meant it could hit us if we didn't go fast enough to get onto the platform. Plus, we had no idea if other trains were on the way or from which direction.

That was our chance, our only chance. We had to decide quickly. Bernie lifted me down to the field where the tracks were located. I had two canes but I couldn't walk fast enough. The taxi driver came with us across the tracks carrying our backpack and our camera, putting himself in danger. Bernie was carrying the wheelchair and he tried to stay by my side in case I fell, which would have been disastrous. I couldn't think about it right then. *Just GO!*

My heart was pounding; I had never done such an idiotic thing, racing trains. We must have been out of our minds. We were not thinking clearly, how could we have been? The anxiety of the morning coupled with the high heat had turned our brains to mush, plus the innate "fight or flight" system kicks in when one's life is endangered. For a disabled woman, I did pretty well; I pushed myself to my limit trying to move forward as fast as I could.

We were getting close to the platform; people came close to the edge to help me up to safe ground. Bernie and the driver reached the platform. Bernie lifted the wheelchair and put it on the train platform, then jumped back down to help me. I was pushed and pulled up onto the platform. I didn't recall too much after that. I was close to passing out; I was in a lot of pain. It was the kind of pain where I "hit the wall", my body and brain had had enough. I passed out just for seconds but it seemed forever. The muscles around my back, stomach, upper chest, and diaphragm were shot. I could barely breathe let alone talk. I finally drank some refreshing water as my head and body normalized.

Through my foggy brain came the sounds of a loud low rumbling and the ground shook. Then I heard hundreds of elephants trumpeting. At first the sound was quiet, then louder. I looked up at and asked Bernie if he heard the same thing. Thankfully, he said yes. I would have thought I was really losing it if he said no. The elephants were on parade. Looking far up the tracks, we saw the elephants walking through a train crossing. There were hundreds of them, including little ones walking one after the other, trunk to tail. We were too far away to take photos. It didn't matter; I was in heaven listening to the elephants communicating with each other. Suddenly, I was completely at peace. Somehow these giant pachyderms pushed my anxiety away. Moments like this change my way of thinking, of acting and listening. I felt so connected — perhaps spiritual — at that moment; I have never forgotten the feeling of total bliss and connectedness to nature. It was a new nature, one far removed from the nature I experienced back home. Something changed in a whole new profound way. A life altering experience: I felt completely calm, not overwhelmed any longer. A wee bit of nirvana.

CHAPTER 21

Huay Thap Than

Certainly, travel is more than the seeing of sights; it's a change that goes on deep and permanent, in the ideas of living.

— Miriam Beard

I was ready for the next experience; visiting a small village in Sisaket Province and meeting our foster girl and family.

The train we took to Huay Thap Than was located half-way between Surin and the town of Sisaket. From that point the two men; one a driver, the other a translator, would drive us to the village. First class" on Thai trains is relative; we were afraid to touch anything so we sat and took in the view out the dirty windows of the train or read our books to pass the time. I saw dry, dusty fields with water buffalo grazing on the small amount of vegetation as we flew by. We saw a few temples and homes here and there. Black electric wires hung in a hodgepodge manner at various road junctions. It didn't look safe. They were strange sites to see: Bernie said "We're not in Kansas anymore." I quickly agreed with him.

The district of Isaan where our foster girl's village was located was one of the poorest areas of the country with an average income of 400 dollars per year.

We arrived in Huay Thap Than, disembarked the train and looked around in search of the two men driving us to the village. They were already there waiting.

The translator spoke excellent English. He had long, grey hair tied back in a ponytail; he had lighter skin than most Thais. We learned later he was from Ubon Ratchathani and was part Laotian. Our driver was definitely Thai and spoke only a little English. Due to obvious differences, they spotted us right away. We climbed into the back seat of the newer truck and headed out.

First, we stopped at a small grocery store in the small town of Huay Thap Than to purchase food for our lunch with the foster family. We had been told by the charity not to buy anything, the family would feed us lunch. We didn't care one way or the other so we bought several items at the store including toothbrushes, laundry soap for the school children and their families, and chicken for our lunch. The total was very inexpensive when converted to dollars. I didn't understand the charity's policy of not buying items for the family; after all, the family was very poor and lived in a village far from the nearest town. How could they be expected to feed us when feeding themselves was difficult at the best of times?

The truck had good suspension, but soon after we made a turn off the main road to the unpaved road leading to the village, the ride got rugged. The driver tried his best to miss craters in the road, nevertheless we were tossed and turned, colliding with each other in the back seat.

People in Isaan maintained tradition and culture. Thais living in this area were primarily Laotian mixed with Thai and Cambodian. About ninety-five percent of the population was Buddhist.

Telephone poles and wires dissected the deep-blue sky. There was electricity to most of the region, gas was used for cooking. It seemed every Thai household had a large flat-screen TV. No matter how poor, there was television.

We passed fields of rice and fields for cows and water buffalo. I felt like Alice in Wonderland falling through the rabbit hole to a shift in time and place. Bernie and I had no idea what to expect or what a village near the Laos/Cambodian border would look like. We had crossed over a century or two of time into the past.

The village was small, maybe fifty houses of disparate styles. Some houses were newer than others, made from cement and painted white — sturdy through any storm nature may bring. Some were basic shelters made from plywood, on stilts. A huff and a puff and blow you right down type dwellings.

The disparity of houses suggested a hierarchy. Most houses gave shelter to three generations; children, parents and at least one set of grandparents. Aunts and uncles may have lived there also.

The house where our foster girl and family lived was one of the largest homes in the village. It was made from wood, had a tin roof, and was built on tall stilts. The house looked to be in good shape; we never saw the inside.

Underneath the house was similar to a large unpaved carport, with some shelter from the sun and wind. It was the place to eat and rest in the shade.

The family and important village men were waiting for us under the stilted house. Bernie and I felt a little nervous initially. Nobody was smiling. Our interpreter introduced us to all the family members, a couple of aunts, uncles, grandparents, as well as the village leader. It seemed like most of the village was crammed under the house in the shaded area. The temperature that day reached 38 degrees Celsius, normal for this area in November. Bernie and I greeted each person as Thai people do, palms pressed together, chest level as if praying, head bent down to touch or almost touch your hands, while you say "*Sawadee ka*" if you are a woman or "*Sawadee krub*" for men.

Most villagers had never seen Caucasian people, let alone one in a wheelchair. Some villagers walked by the house, taking a look at what all the fuss was about. I couldn't blame people for staring, but when I glanced in their direction, their eyes quickly looked down; eye contact with a newcomer was rude.

Smiling for a photo didn't work here. It was a solemn event. We were the" esteemed guests." Bernie and I are more humble than gregarious in our demeanor and life; we felt uncomfortable being placed in a situation of honour or esteem. We were a glass wedding-couple on top of cake and it was definitely hard to get our heads around. At home we earned a moderately good living. We lived fairly quietly enjoying our surroundings in the country.

Our eyes became adjusted to the shadows and the dust under the house. I looked around trying to guess who was who. I recognized the family from photos we had been sent. The people here had extraordinary features, especially the elderly. I noticed a woman who was elderly but I couldn't even guess what age she might be. Her face was deeply grooved by wrinkles, years of hardship, living in desert conditions and raising a family in constant poverty. Guessing the age of Thai people was challenging; the young and middle-aged looked very young, the older Thais looked ancient. I spotted a very old man lying on a mat on a different table than where we sat. *Is he dead'?* He didn't look alive. He hadn't moved a breath since we arrived but about an hour later, just before lunch he was suddenly on his feet. Glaucoma clouded his eyes to smoky-blue; he stood not much higher than my own five feet. His grey hair was askew like a munchkin or troll doll. It appeared most Thais didn't grow to high heights, due to nutritional deficits. I had yet to see an overweight man or woman. It would have been difficult to get fat on their non-existing salaries and mostly vegetarian diet.

This family worked in rice fields, planting and harvesting. They owned a cow or water buffalo; I didn't get a chance to see where the animal was kept in a nearby field.

Often, the Thai mothers and fathers moved to the southern beaches of Thailand to work for several months during their non-farming time, in restaurants, in the resorts, or stores. Just a few years ago our foster girl's parents travelled south every year to secure jobs for the tourist season. Her parents did not usually work in the same city. Separated by impoverishment, her mother and father went wherever they could to find a job, usually in the south. They would return to the village in time to harvest or sow rice. Fortunately, they were able to save enough money to buy a cow and some land for grazing.

No matter how poor many Thais were, there was an undertone of happiness floating around just below the surface — including kids who have almost nothing. Kids being kids, they found a way to play whatever the setting may be.

I asked our interpreter "What do people in small villages do for entertainment; do they play card games, other games or read books?" He had a look on his face that told me he didn't understand what I asked. I was surprised, his English was excellent. I tried again: "What do people do, aside from school and work? What do the villagers do for fun?" Still looking a little perplexed, his answer was "Watch TV." Simple as that.

Three young girls made sure we always had coconut juice, straight from the coconut. Delicious: we drank from a straw inserted in the coconut husk. As soon as our shell was near empty they took it away and opened more coconuts for us to drink. Both of our heads were spinning, drunk on coconut juice. Husks were strewn around the yard like empty beer bottles at a college party. We tried to tell them "No more," but they kept coming. We kept drinking the juice slowly. We had watched the TV show *Survivor* back home and couldn't believe how many times the participants declared there was no water or food. Crack open a coconut, drink the juice and scrape out the "meat" inside: it will keep you from starving and dehydration.

Our foster girl plus some cousins and friends arrived from school. They were on their lunch break. They were shy at first then a bit giggly, just like young girls everywhere. We handed out the presents we bought for the foster family. They went crazy over the soccer ball, and mom received a pretty silk scarf, dad a baseball cap, and there was a doll for our foster girl. There were several items for the family and school. Soap, laundry detergent, toothbrushes, and other sundries were much appreciated.

While lunch was being made it was suggested that we take a walk around the village. It didn't take long. Bernie pushed me in the wheelchair; the "road" was mostly dirt. The main road went around the village with a couple of roads dissecting the square. It took about ten minutes to see everything. We took a lot of photos hoping to convey village life in rural Thailand to show to family and friends back home.

As we walked around the village we met almost everyone who lived there except the children who were having lunch at school. We met young parents and old ones, and peeked at little babies snug in cotton sashes, wrapped around mom's shoulder.

The slim-gin chickens crowed, piercing our eardrums with their cackle, and ran like the dickens in front or beside us, stirring up reddish soil as they sought haven. We also saw a few rangy goats; one was wandering the streets attempting to butt us. Lucky for me I was in the wheelchair.

Thailand was having a general election: when we were in Bangkok we saw pick-up trucks with large candidate placards tied on each side and men yelling through a microphone to vote for this candidate or that one. Bangkok was noisy and the announcements were lost in traffic sounds. In the city it was a mild irritant; hearing the same type of trucks in the village was deafening. Fortunately, they left after driving a few (hundred) times around the village. After pounding their message into everyone's head they left us stunned. The ensuing silence was deafening.

As we strolled around we met several other people of the village, adults and children. Our interpreter asked us if we would like to see the school later and a visit was arranged for after lunch.

In North America most people wash their hands before eating, especially if their hands have dirt and grime on them, as ours did from our day so far, including the long train ride. I asked our interpreter where we could wash our hands before we ate — oh, oh a major faux pas for Bernie and me! Soon one of the women brought us a small bowl of water which was poured over our hands. There was no towel; we shook off the excess water. We were being watched by the extended family and volunteers from Plan Thailand. Later our interpreter explained the villagers treat water as gold. The charity provided huge cisterns to the village to collect rainfall and use it for cleaning and cooking; rain was scarce especially in this dry climate and water was not always available.

We were led to the picnic table under the house in the shade. We were provided with two small bowls with rice in each and one spoon, the type you may see in a Chinese restaurant. Not knowing all the customs regarding food etiquette we assumed the rice in the bowls were for us to eat. We sat there for a minute or two not knowing what to do; more food had been brought in but nobody had begun serving or eating. Everyone was seated either on the picnic table benches, on the picnic table, or on the ground. Our interpreter told us to start. Bernie and I didn't realize we were to eat food using our hands. We used the Chinese style spoon and asked for another. We each had a bowl and now two spoons. We added some fish to our bowls; one fish had been prepared in very hot spices, and it brought tears to my eyes. I made a point to remember not to wipe my eyes with my hands. Chicken and another type of fish arrived at the table in old bowls, a vegetable soup of designs.

The Thai people must have wondered what the heck we were doing keeping all the rice to ourselves. Nobody laughed, nobody gasped. Bernie and I had thought we had asked our Thai tutor back home every question we could think of regarding this visit to a small village in the middle of nowhere. He supplied information on many of the customs we hadn't thought to ask about. I guess we missed one or two things — we didn't ask about the villagers' eating habits. More rice arrived at the table for everyone to partake, well except for Bernie and me, we had plenty.

We watched as the rest of the people started eating using their right hands to scoop a small ball of sticky rice. Then with the rice ball, they scooped some meat and sauce from the fish or chicken dishes, then popped it in their mouths. Yum-yum. Everything was amazingly delicious. Knowing the people here had very little money to buy chicken and fish, Bernie and I ate a good amount of food to express our thanks, but not too much. We didn't want to take more food from the family — we already had eaten their rice.

We finished lunch and all were satisfied. Our foster girl needed to get back to school and away she went on the back of dad's motor scooter, a popular mode of transportation all over Thailand. We took pictures of everyone, including the village chief, administrators, and volunteers from the charity. We didn't want to leave but we were expected at the school at 2:00. Bernie and I said our goodbyes, in Thai, of course. What an incredible visit we had. An experience like no other, transporting us back in time to a simple way of life, but not an easy one. It was a cruel life in extreme conditions where rain was unpredictable and often caused flooding, wiping out vegetation, rice fields, and even worse, affecting access to healthy drinking water or wiping out whole villages. Most, but not all houses were built on stilts, some higher than others; some were built with bricks that withstood any storm, but there were still too many living below the poverty line in cardboard boxes or flimsy lean-tos made from thin plywood with a make-shift tin roof.

It was difficult to grasp and hold onto the events of the day so far: to figure out what these events meant to Bernie and me. Right then my head was reeling; I couldn't process how I felt about anything at that moment.

We said our goodbyes, climbed into the truck and drove the dusty red road to the children's school. The school was larger than I thought it would be; I hadn't taken into account all the other villages' children. The rustic school had two levels and taught grades one to twelve.

As soon as we got out of the truck we were surrounded by smiling children — well, most were — some held back looking through suspicious eyes. I'd be doing the same thing if I had never seen a Caucasian man and woman, let alone one in a wheelchair — a contraption never seen before by these villagers. The disabled in Thailand, of which there are many I'm sure, are not seen in public. Many Thai still have suspicions regarding the disabled: they were the useless, the brainless. I hope things have changed in the past ten years.

It wasn't that many years ago in North America that disabled people were seen as having a low IQ, making able bodied people uncomfortable. Let's thank Rick Hansen for his bravery, wheeling across Canada, from sea to shining sea.

In 1980 Rick Hansen's predecessor, Terry Fox, started his odyssey *The Marathon of Hope,* running fearlessly across Canada raising public awareness of the disabled and raising money for cancer research. He had one good leg used an artificial leg for the other. His "run-hop" style of mobility was famous across the land. His attempt to cross Canada came to an end some 143 days and 5,373 kilometres later; Terry had to stop his dream of hope.

In 1980 Rick Hansen's *Man in Motion Tour* took twenty-six months to wheel from shore to shore across mountains and through valleys of rugged Canada, raising awareness of disability and money for spinal cord injuries research. Because of their bravery they have brought disability out of the closet giving disabled dignity and hope. We are now seen everywhere, at least in North America.

My thoughts drifted back to the children in the school; hearing their laughter while they played and watching as they chased each other around the school yard. Hide-and-seek was popular. The school-bell rang and all of the kids quickly lined up one by one. It was time to brush their teeth. I was fascinated at the unique method to help kids stay healthy.

Each child had their own toothbrush, some toothpaste, and a cup with water to rinse. Now I understood why we had bought so many toothbrushes and toothpaste at the grocery store we stopped at before we drove to the village. It was a gift for the school.

The children, little soldiers all in a line, waited for the signal to start brushing and keep brushing for three minutes. The teacher called a halt; the children stopped brushing, took a mouthful of water, turned to the right and spat in unison in the dirt. The majority of the kids wore school uniforms with a few exceptions. I turned to our interpreter, "Why do some children not wear uniforms?" He turned to the vice principal, who had arrived at the school yard a short time ago, and asked him. The answer, he told me, was because there weren't enough uniforms for every child, even though they were passed down to the kids in the lower grade from the higher grade at the end of school. I felt a sadness I'd not felt before. It was the poorer kids who didn't have a uniform; their families could not afford to purchase one. Being a mother myself, I grieved for these children. I shook my head as I thought of the kids back home, the ones who had everything they needed or wanted. I couldn't help thinking about North America's penchant for spoiling kids and teaching them to be materialistic adults like themselves. We all should be ashamed.

The bell rang and the children scrambled to their classrooms. Bernie, me, our interpreter, and the vice principal continued to chat. The VP asked, through our interpreter, if we would like to see a classroom. Of course we would.

We approached the classroom where our foster girl was sitting with her classmates. It was a small room, enough for a dozen kids. The desks were a disparate selection of sizes and colours; some students sat at a long wooden table, others at individual desks pushed together. They all sat on hard wooden chairs. When my eyes adjusted to the dim light I had a better look inside the classroom. The children sat still, most with a blank look on their faces and only one girl was smiling, our foster girl. The teacher came to the door to say hello to us (*Sawadee krub*).

I didn't see textbooks, paper, or other items usually found in a classroom. I asked if they had these implements. After much discussion between our interpreter, the VP and the teacher, we were informed that the village schools could not afford notebooks, pencils, erasers, chalk, and textbooks. The children were allotted half of a pencil and a few pieces of paper twice a year. There was only one textbook and this had to be shared with other classes. The poor teacher only had a quarter piece of chalk, that's it.

Bernie and I were truly shocked. How would any of these children get an education? If they lived in a city in Thailand and went to a private school they would receive a good education with abundant supplies until grade 12, and have many advantages over kids living in poor areas. The education department of the government controlled what supplies each school in a region would receive. There was a lot of corruption in Thailand so it was probable that some districts received less school supplies due to pilfering or bribes from the wealthier areas.

During our second trip to Thailand we learned much more about the many problems of the education system and a year and a half later, We met an English speaker teacher who was living in Sisaket. He had a lot to say on the subject. His frustration at the system was palpable. He knew what went on in rural schools. We had interesting conversations in the morning over coffee.

It was getting late in the afternoon and we had a train to meet. Our Thai driver took us to the station. We said our heartfelt thanks to our driver and interpreter. Once we got home we would send letters with photos and a few CDs to both of our volunteers. Excellent people.

We were very exhausted at the end of our visit. Our minds were spinning; all we wanted now was to be back at the hotel to have a snooze.

The train that took us back to Surin didn't have a class system to it (1st, 2nd, or 3rd). The train was full of workers returning from the fields and stores. The train was old and filthy. We sat ourselves in the only two seats we could find, right beside a very stinky toilet. We had to breathe through our mouths all the way back to Surin, over an hour. It was almost comparable to the trains in India, heavily stacked high with people, goats and chickens. We didn't take any photos; we might have been tossed off the train if we did.

Bernie had to stow my wheelchair in the next compartment. I was concerned someone might walk away with it. I'm was having trust issues at that moment.

Why, I wasn't sure. I knew I was exhausted from our jammed-packed day. Nobody on the train had given me any reason to be wary. As a matter of fact, our entire trip to Thailand was uneventful regarding theft. I was normally very perceptive; I read people very well, at home anyway. I pick on the nuances of strangers, whether I might be in danger or not: it's part of my fight or flight survival method. This also comes from being a nurse; we must have a sixth sense when evaluating patients, to be able to read their bodies for signs of pain, fear, confusion, and anger. It has saved me from harm many times.

I realized later, after resting for a few days, the majority of Thai people were very helpful, quick to lend a hand, happy to help. I may have been stared at frequently but I never felt in danger.

I've been suffering for a long time, since I was a child. My beliefs have been challenged throughout the years. I've researched many religions and have come to my own conclusions. I spent a decade attending an evangelical church, but after my first husband and I moved we started at a sister church where I became disillusioned with many "Christians." After we were divorced I was informed I would not be able to marry again in the church. Really! I left with my three kids. I did try a couple other churches but soon realized each and everyone was absolutely adamant they were the correct church/faith to follow. I gave up.

The last few years I've refocused my beliefs. Bernie has been through a few Buddhist silent meditation retreats in Southeast Asia. He has vocalized, to me, his understanding of Buddhist practice. This has prompted me to search further into Buddhism. I wondered, *Am I missing answers to my perplexing, complicated life?*. I continued researching. Science has completely won me over: that, and trying to be a decent person and fit into society.

We arrived at the train station in Surin, exhausted and grimy, back to reality, in this country where nothing seemed real to us.

We took a tuk-tuk, as we did when we first arrived in Surin, back to our hotel; it took less than five minutes; a far cry from our experience that morning. The hotel was packed full; we could hardly make it around people, just about all tourists, to the hotel's only elevator. *Phew!* We made it into our room safe and sound. We took turns having a refreshing shower then went to sleep as soon as we laid our heads on the pillow.

Tomorrow would be another big day: the Surin Elephant Festival. After our three hour snooze we embarked on another walk through Surin and found an outdoor restaurant — more like a portable stove that was boxy and silver. There were four plastic tables and chairs. We had our pick; there were no other clients. We each ordered a chicken and noodle dish. As usual it was very good, mouth watering. We were very thirsty, so we ordered mango juice. It came over ice. Hmmm. I remembered that classic travel advice, "Do not drink the water or anything with ice." It was very easy to get infected with water-born bacteria. That was the last thing we needed. We drank the juice, ice and all, and hoped we wouldn't regret it.

CHAPTER 22

The Elephant Festival

Be willing to be uncomfortable. Be comfortable being uncomfortable. It may get tough, but it's a small price to pay for living a dream.
— Peter McWilliams

We went to sleep early that night and were up at 6:30. I could barely get out of bed. I felt so weak. How am I going to get through this day? Half my brain was screaming at me, *Stay in bed, it's not worth it!* while the other half was yelling, barely above the first half, *You can do it, you have come all this way, you cannot miss the elephant festival!* I got up, took my medication, dressed, and went downstairs for a quick breakfast. There was a self-serve continental breakfast consisting of juice — mango, we thought — coffee, toast, or muffins. Good enough for the time being. All of the hotel guests were transported in vans or shuttle buses to the stadium where the festival was held.

Bernie had purchased VIP tickets for the Elephant Festival when he booked the hotel; this meant we would have a seat somewhere on the metal bleachers under the overhang. Others were seated directly in the sun. Our shuttle took us to the gates of the stadium. We still had to walk down a road to the actual stadium. Hundreds of elephants with their trainers were everywhere down the length of that road. We walked with elephants large and small. Many were standing on the grass nearby waiting for their part in the show. On top of each of the older and much larger elephants was a basket, called a *howdah*, holding the trainers. They both were regal, showing the king's colours, rich with pomp and circumstance. I was in heaven. I must have been dreaming. If so, then I didn't want to wake up. *Let me finish my unbelievable prehistoric illusions.* Things would be real enough when we returned home.

We sat about half-way up the bleachers in our designated metal seats. There were two couples from the States sitting beside and behind us. They looked to be close to the same age as Bernie and I. Between the three couples, there was a paramedic, x-ray technician, an emergency room nurse, and me, an all-round RN. If there were some type of disaster, we had everything covered medically. Thank goodness nothing went wrong.

The pageant began. The setting was proudly regal. Thai music started and into the stadium marched the big elephants and the little elephants, connected tail to trunk. They swayed side to side, lumbering through the side entrance, walking directly in front of us. Beautiful Thai women paraded in after the elephants across to the other end of the stadium. There were as many trainers as elephants walking close by, just in case the elephants decided to keep on walking to the South China Sea. The stadium must have been football-sized to hold three hundred elephants and as many people, all with their roles in the pageant.

The pageant took the audience back to the reign of King Rama II (King of Siam) in the early 1800s. He was known as an artist and wood carving was his passion; he also liked to write and compose. During his reign he had many temples (*wats*) built, as well as a general reconstruction of Siamese culture.

For centuries, the people of Surin were renowned for their ability to capture and train elephants. The Ban Ta Klang elephant village, located in Surin Province, is home to the Kui who migrated from Cambodia or Laos to Northeastern Thailand (Isaan). The majority of elephant owners or trainers (Mahout) are descendants of the Kui.

The elephants, or chang, were respected and revered by kings. Elephants were treated as family members. They were a symbol of power and grace. Abuse, however, has been reported recently; bull-hooks or *ancas* continue to be used on sensitive areas on the elephant's body. The *mahouts* use the bull-hooks for control and discipline. The elephants are also used for work, hauling logs, pulling out stumps, and more. The work is difficult and exhausting for the elephants. They work in 35 degree Celsius heat with high humidity.

The Elephant Festival recreated battle scenes from the reign of King Rama II. There were also competition scenes, demonstrations of warfare techniques, and a tug-of-war between the *mahouts* wearing their battlefield outfits from the Thai, Khmer and Laos battles.

There were demonstrations of elephant talents: a few elephants were "painting" pictures standing on their front legs; this, unfortunately, reminded me of animals in a circus. At one point there must have been a few hundred elephants on the stadium field. Bernie and I were captivated. We couldn't stop taking photos and videos. It was a jammed-packed experience; I loved the gentle beasts. Some of the elephants were absolutely humongous; there was a lot of trumpeting going on. We saw a few little ones being guarded by a couple of older female elephants. The young ones were so sweet with a little bit of hair on their heads.

The show went on for two or three hours. Several years later it seems like a dream but I know we were there; I have pictures.

An older woman to the left of me was sitting beside the aisle. One of the American couples was beside Bernie; the other couple was behind them. I chatted with the older woman, discovering she was Swedish. Numerous times throughout the show an older man, tall and lean with sparse grey hair, would descend the stairs coughing like he was ready to die. He would stay at the bottom of the bleachers for a while. I didn't pay attention to him at first, I was so busy talking to the people next to us and watching the show. Several more times he ascended and descended the bleachers coughing as if his lungs were turning inside-out. I thought he might have a heart attack any minute; his face kept going purple. The grey-haired lady — the one right beside the aisle — and I kept looking at each other with concern on our faces wondering why the man was even present at the festival if he was so sick. We shook our heads a couple times then went back to watching the show. There were tourists from all over the globe present that day, a melting pot of cultures and languages and germs.

Too soon the pageant finished. We said goodbye to our new friends from the States.

After the pageant, elephant rides were offered and although I had to climb stairs to a tall platform to get into the carriage on top of the elephant, I gladly would have had Bernie fling me over his shoulder and carry me up. I made it on my own. I couldn't believe we didn't get a photo of us riding on top of the elephant, but the memory is as clear as the day of the pageant. I can still feel the gentle swaying of the elephant as he walked around the large stadium.

Just outside the stadium, elephants with their *mahouts* were moseying along, drunk with fun of the day. There were hundreds of elephants sauntering about without a care in the world. Some were so enormous I felt like a pip-squeak, all five feet of me sitting in my wheelchair.

Bernie suggested we check out the trade show happening next to the stadium. It was large and took us nearly an hour to walk through. We bought a couple of silly items for the grandkids and a T-shirt or so. Both of us were exhausted from our day; we hadn't had time to catch up on our sleep from the previous hectic days.

CHAPTER 23

Ubon Ratchathani (Lotus City)

Travelling, it leaves you speechless, then turns you into a storyteller.

— Ibn Battuta

We were sad to leave the elephants and Surin behind; it was time to move on to our next destination: Ubon Ratchathani, the most eastern province in Thailand.

My pain level was through the roof and I was very exhausted: the story of my life. The train ride to Ubon Ratchathani took two hours, just enough time to relax and read for a bit. The train was, to my surprise, old but clean; was it my imagination or had I accepted the fact of travel in Thailand?

The countryside was flat and dry. There were some scattered trees and watering holes for water buffalo, a wooden house here and there. The train windows were caked with fine reddish sand; not the best for picture taking. Any small movement on the land caused a tornado of dirt to swirl through the air, indiscriminately blanketing nearby objects, trees, vehicles, and people. There were no clean cars here and no clean laundry. Although some people owned clothes dryers more often you would see laundry hanging outdoors to save money on energy consumption.

As the train rumbled ahead, houses began to pop up closer together, melding into the city of Ubon Ratchathani (aka Ubon), population 122,533. The city and the province are both named Ubon Ratchathani. People who have settled here are descendants from the Khmer of Cambodia as well as Laos and Vietnam. Ubon Ratchathani has many ex-pats from the US; many settled in Ubon after the Vietnam War, and there used to be a US armed forces unit in Ubon.

Many people waved at the train in greeting, smiles on every face. Even the field workers took a moment to wave hello and welcome. Some workers were dressed in cool cotton clothes while others were covered head to toe in shirts, sweaters, long pants, and large hats with a scarf around the neck. November is a cooler month for people living here; we were plenty hot in the dry 32 degrees Celsius temperature in the shade.

Ubon Ratchathani had the highest concentration of temples, or *wats* in Thailand. Some were very old and made from wood, while other *wats* were brilliant white with gold domes on top. They resembled a reverse ice cream cone, which would have been nice to have had right then. I was covered in sweat. I wondered if ice cream cones existed there. Possibly, but we hadn't seen any so far.

Along with the many temples, monks were abundant and dressed in orange sarongs. There were old monks and young; there were 460,000 monks in 32,000 *wats* at that time. There were a lot of shades of saffron floating around Thailand. I always loved to see the young boys pouring out of their classes in temples. Their shrieks of laughter and boyish antics were no different than what I had seen at home when elementary school let out for recess.

We disembarked the train ready for more adventure, hopefully a tad less hectic.

Again we took a tuk-tuk which we barely fit in with the wheelchair, camera bag, clothing bag, and Bernie's long legs. There was never enough room for his legs.

Like Bangkok, Ubon Ratchathani had a significant contrast in living standards. As we approached the train station earlier we saw many people living in huts just on the other side of the railway tracks, some with fruit stands. Other parts of the city had apartment buildings where the working class lived and although we didn't explore the entire city I was sure there was a wealthy class of homes — somewhere behind bars, usually.

Our hotel was very pretty and clean. Unfortunately we were on the second floor and there wasn't an elevator. There weren't any rooms on the first floor, just the restaurant and front desk. I felt bad for Bernie, hauling the backpack and the wheelchair up the stairs, but he did it over and over as we came and went.

I rested, or tried to, and Bernie went searching for information and a driver so we could explore some of the *wats* and see the mighty Mekong River the next day.

Later we went downstairs for dinner. We didn't feel like venturing out so the hotel restaurant seemed an easy place to be. In Taipei there were plastic molds of the food on the menu to look at and help us make a choice. Here the menu had plenty of photos beside the Thai writing so foreigners, like us, could point to what we wanted to order. It was still a crapshoot of what might be served.

Feeling better and a little livelier after some good food in our bellies we set out for a walk. I was still in pain and very exhausted but still it was nice to be outdoors. Bernie seemed to think this town was looking wheelchair-friendly and in a way it was. There were several areas along the sidewalk near the street corners that were level with the street, like a driveway, but these were for delivery carts. I still hadn't seen one regular wheelchair anywhere, just a man being pulled on a small wheeled platform by a young boy in Bangkok. These dips in the sidewalk made our ventures outdoors much easier. We certainly had a lot of people staring at us. A big, tall Caucasian man with a tiny woman in a wheelchair. I really didn't like the attention.

Along the way we passed a video store. The TV was on in the front window and one of the Harry Potter movies was on and blaring Thai over English. There were several young and older men watching the movie intently. It sure was loud.

On our walk back to the hotel the movie had finished and the men had left. There were two very young girls; one was a toddler, maybe three years old and the other maybe five, sitting on the sidewalk holding a doll — but it wasn't a doll at all but a baby. One of the girls jumped up and held an empty cup towards us. It broke my heart.

Everywhere we had explored in Thailand there were beggars of all descriptions, mainly children and the infirm elderly. It was a slap across the face to wake up to what we had read in books: to actually see such poverty was difficult to get our heads around.

Almost all the children were small for their age. Our foster girl was nine years old but was as small as a six or seven-year-old North American child. When we walked around the village we saw a young couple holding a child in their arms. I thought the child was maybe ten to twelve months old but when I asked our interpreter, he said the child was actually three years old. There wasn't enough protein and other nutrients in their diets as the children grew.

We had a great sleep from 10:30 to 6:30. We certainly were not early risers but outside our hotel window another candidate truck with very large speakers was blaring information on their favoured election candidate. Did they really need to have their speakers blaring full blast? It scared the living daylights out of us more than once, especially this early in the morning. I thought we were under attack or there was a tsunami warning. It took a few minutes to shake off our sleepiness and figure out that it was only the political trucks playing their message at a full crescendo shaking all of the nearby buildings, our hotel included.

There were many people up and already working. A construction crew was buzzing and hammering next door. Across the street the market was being set up and many carts full of goods were being hauled to one of the many tables under awnings. It was a large market. We even saw a few Catholic nuns doing some very early shopping for vegetables and what-not.

After breakfast we headed out. Dust didn't settle under our feet for long. What a fantastic day it was. I loved the weather here. It was a bit cooler than Sisaket and Surin, as Ubon is closer to the Mekong and Mun rivers.

We toured a good part of the city that we could see by walking. We saw a couple of lovely parks and statues and many *wats*. Most of the *wats* we had seen thus far on our trip were very ornate: always clean, painted gold, red, and blue. Some had pieces of shiny tin or mirrors to give the *wat* a sparkling look.

We came upon a very old *wat*, made of wood, not ornate at all. We passed a few monks out for a walk and lo and behold one turned to us and in English asked where we were from. We hadn't heard much English in this town, especially without a strong Thai accent. I'm sure we looked as shocked as we had when we met Simon in his wheelchair in Taiwan.

It turned out this monk came from Australia. Between his accent and his face, he looked like an Australian aboriginal. He had the biggest smile and peacefulness radiated all around him.

We never did catch his name. He claimed he had been a "very bad boy" in Australia until a friend there led him to the teachings of Buddha. It was his first year as a full can't-turn-back monk. He claimed the first three months of training were the most difficult for him. Training to be a monk was long and arduous; it took total acceptance to leave a world where money rules. He seriously glowed. The love poured out of him. When he spoke about leaving his old ways behind and finding joy, serenity and the spirit of giving, his face lit up. He was happy to stop and chat in

English with us. He walked with us and told us the history of the wooden *wat*.

Wat Thung Si Muang, the simple, unadorned small wooden wat, was far more significant than it appeared. It had been built in the early 1800s to house a replica of the Buddha's footprint.

The plain-looking wooden *wat* built was on stilts in a lotus pond. The water was to protect the wooden library inside from insects such as termites.

The library in that *wat* contained the *Tripitaka Scriptures* written on palm leaves. Each leaf had been perforated and sewn and combined in stacks of twenty to forty pages, then wrapped and pressed between wooden teak planks.

At some point in history the scriptures were sold to the Japanese and were to be removed from this *wat* and sent to Japan. When the people of Ubon heard about this transaction and the potential loss of such sacred texts they protested loudly and the scriptures were left in place. The Japanese would not take back the money paid and each year many Japanese travel to Ubon Ratchathani to pay homage. We couldn't believe how fortunate we were at having almost walked right into this monk from Australia. His knowledge was astounding to us, as was the fact that this old, almost unadorned *wat* held ancient scriptures. That reminded me not to judge a book by its cover.

The other *wat* the monk pointed out had a statue of Buddha that was thought to be made of plaster, as many were under their gilded outer layer. When the statue was to be moved to another location, a piece of plaster fell off and revealed a solid silver Buddha underneath. Utterly amazing — I'd always been fascinated by a country's history.

We could have chatted with him for hours but his companion didn't speak English and was trying very hard not to look impatient. He wasn't coming across as a tranquil monk. Maybe he had to use the loo.

I'm happy we had been able to speak with the monk from Australia because after observing other older monks around the city, they didn't seem too happy. The Thai people were always ready to help us without asking. At times Bernie would try and wave them off. The wheelchair needed to be lifted a certain way when I was seated so the legs wouldn't pop off, but sometimes the Thai people were so anxious and happy to help it was hard to say no. The monks never helped even when there were no other people around. One even turned his back on me. Maybe he was having a bad day but most likely it was because I was female.

It was an educational and fun walk-about.

Through our hotel, Bernie found a driver to give us a tour the next day of more *wats* on the way to see the mighty Mekong River. We were both really looking forward to having a guide who also spoke some English.

We didn't have air conditioning in any of our lodgings, but it usually cooled in the evening when a light breeze would blow through the room. It had been a hot night but we slept well and I even felt ok the next morning — until I had breakfast.

My stomach was very painful right after eating and our driver had just arrived. There was a toilet on the main floor near the restaurant where we were but it was recently vacated and stunk to high heaven. My stomach started roiling. I started sweating and feeling dizzy, very dizzy, and nauseated. Bernie had gone to speak with the driver. I grabbed the room key and ran for the stairs; holding onto the railing to pull myself up the two levels. I kept getting dizzier and dizzier. There wasn't carpeting on the floors. It was an old building that had marble floors and stairs and I was worried if I did faint I might end up with a concussion, or worse.

I struggled to open the room door and remain conscious. I finally got the door open and ran for the bed where I promptly passed out for an hour. That was a very frightening experience. I never did vomit and after I woke up I was good-to-go. I initially thought it was food poisoning but if so, then it sure passed quickly. I never knew what to expect with my health. The same thing has happened to me several times over the years. I often never know when or why.

Bernie had to re-negotiate with the driver as he had sent him away as we both had thought I was down for the rest of the day. The drive was great on the way to Kong Chiam, the road was smooth, and the windows were clean, so sight-seeing from inside the car was good.

Along the way we stopped at a few *wats*. Our first stop was the #1 Wat; that really was its name. It was impressive and huge. There were three other *wats* nearby, each decorated differently from the other. One *wat* was adorned in sparkling silver, difficult to stare at when the sun was shining as it always seemed to in Thailand, especially in that dry desert area.

The biggest *wat* we saw, Heo Sin Chai, was the most intriguing. We had to walk down several stairs to the *sala*, or main area of the temple, as opposed to the majority of *wats* where we walked in or up several stairs. I always brought my cane for times when I couldn't use the wheelchair. This *wat* was underground, so after descending the many stairs, which I did get down, we entered a cave. I was very curious to see what was located here. Candles had been lit and placed in sconces to guide our way.

There were small-to-medium-sized statues of monks on shelves along the walls. Each was painted a different colour. The driver had told us there was a sarcophagus in the cave but I don't remember seeing it. There were several people and kids leaving small gifts and praying at the back of the cave. Apparently there was a waterfall near the cave but we were in the dry season and it was also dry. Too bad, it was supposed to be amazing in the rainy season.

I had stairs to climb to get back up to ground level. I would have thought it would be cooler in the cave but it was hot and humid. I needed to get out quickly; I was getting dizzy again.

We climbed up and down stairs for all the *wats* we had seen on our trip, except for the small wooden *wat* in the lotus pond. I was getting my exercise; if I hadn't gained a lot of strength in my leg, hip, and pelvic muscles by the time we got home, then there truly would be a medical dysfunction of some sort. Anytime in the past when I had gotten sick or sprained an ankle or broken some body part I always bounced back fairly quickly because I never was a girl or woman who wanted to sit still for long. Parts of this trip, I figured, would either kill me or cure me. I was happy seeing a part of the world I had only read about in novels. Expanding my world views and immersing myself for a short while in another culture had been beyond my dreams. Thanks to Bernie for all of our beautiful and challenging trips, learning other languages and cultures. We continued our drive to where the Mekong and the Mun rivers converged. The blue Mun river runs into the brown Mekong at this point of Kong Chiam. There are two distinct colours of water as if a line was drawn between the two.

The Ubon Royal Thai Air Force Base was established in 1950, due to an increasing concern over communists in Laos (pronounced *Lao*) inciting a civil war and spreading into Thailand. During the Vietnam War, the United States was permitted to use the Ubon Royal Thai Air Force Base and four other bases to covertly defend the air-space and fly reconnaissance. As we stood in Kong Chiam, as far east as we could drive in Eastern Thailand, we could see Laos across the river and beyond that lay Vietnam. Asia could be a turbulent area but was very rich in history.

We toured the area for a few hours until it was time to head back to the hotel. There was always something interesting to look at out the window. A large truck was transporting a water buffalo, a huge beast with a large hump on its back and impressive horns. Maybe the man just bought him or the bull had been hired out to stud for all the lonely female buffalo in the fields with the ubiquitous egrets on their backs. The water buffalo were a dying breed in Thailand as many farmers or villages now owned tractors. The poor farms in the central and northern areas of Thailand were too poor to buy tractors, but they had TVs. I've learned that you can't make judgments on how people live their lives. TV can be great escapism.

Another peculiar sight for us was all the small scooters and motorcycles zipping by with usually two to four people aboard. Somehow, the women, when sitting on the back of a scooter, sat side-saddle without holding onto the driver or the scooter, even when going over bumps or around corners. Often enough the woman would be holding a baby in her arms like a football; sometimes we would see a small child perched on the handlebars in front of the driver. One driver was transporting a huge bale of hay, another a four-foot-high white bag of rice, with another a sack full of straw brooms — much taller than he was — strapped on the his back. Amazing balance. Gazing out the window of the car was better than watching TV as far as I was concerned.

Our driver took us back to our hotel in time for dinner. Ubon Ratchathani was an interesting visit. Every night we ordered our dinner in the hotel we were staying in. Not many spoke English there, so every time we ordered dinner it was a crapshoot as to what we would end up eating.

The day after, we decided to venture out for breakfast before our flight back to Bangkok. It was a lazy morning, which was good because after getting in and out of the car so many times the day before and climbing up and down stairs of the *wats* I was in pain and exhausted.

After we checked out of the hotel we sat outside, people-watching. I was determined to take a photo of a family on a scooter, which I did.

The plane ride was very quick back to Bangkok, unlike the eight-to-twelve-hour train ride from Bangkok to Surin. The trains were notoriously late or early, never on time. There was a monk in a brand new orange robe sitting behind us on the small passenger plane and my goodness could he snore!

We returned to the hotel in Bangkok where we had originally stayed and had left our large backpack.

Back to dirty smelly Bangkok; I must have been getting acclimatized because I was delighted to be there. The hotel was beautiful and fairly new. Before we had dinner at the restaurant we went up to the eighty-third floor for a cocktail before dinner. We felt like we were in the clouds. We were so far removed from the squalor of the streets.

We had cloth napkins on our dinner table, real toilets, toilet paper, and Kleenex in the bathrooms, plus lovely sinks and taps. Up north one was lucky to have one small square of TP and usually no napkins, cloth or not, on any table. Often there wasn't a place to wash our hands after using the toilet. I did wonder about the cooks and servers' hand hygiene. I decided not to think about that. As Scarlett O'Hara said, "I'll think about that tomorrow, tomorrow is another day." When we travelled in developing countries with few natural assets such as running water, we had to put our normal hygiene practices aside and try to keep our hands from our faces. Not always easy to do.

I ordered snapper and it arrived at our table with the head, fins, tail, and full skeleton intact. Thank goodness my grandpa taught me to fish, de-head, and debone fish. Bernie had chicken but thankfully it had already been plucked and de-capitated. After dinner I went for an incredible Thai massage that was offered in the hotel spa. I sure hurt horribly but the masseuse really worked out the kinks in my muscles.

The next morning after a great breakfast at the lobby restaurant on the eighteenth floor, I sat and caught up with my journal and Bernie was out looking for a money exchange.

We decided to tour around Bangkok one more time before we headed south. We set out, Bernie walking, me in the chair. We toured several *wats* including Wat Pho, to see the Reclining Golden Buddha in his repose before death, before he reached nirvana.

As we waited in line I could hardly believe my eyes, but there it was the same colourful bird I saw in my dream. Was this some kind of sign? But for what? I had no clue, maybe just an acknowledgement that I had made the right choice to see this astonishing country.

We took another plane — the movie *Planes, Trains and Automobiles* came to mind — this time we flew to Krabi on Thai Air in the southern part of Thailand. We were on our way to the beautiful aqua beaches in the south.

We had an overnight stay in a Krabi hotel. It was horrible. Our room was one floor below ground level and it smelled moldy. It was such a horrible smell that we asked for a different room. There were two rooms available, one on the second floor and one on the fourth. We chose the room on the second floor, but it wasn't much better. The hotel was right on the beach so what did we expect? The humidity was high. There weren't many lodgings to choose from; we just booked that morning from Ubon. We nearly didn't have a spot to stay at all. We didn't know it was summer holidays for children and people were travelling.

The air conditioner in that second room dripped onto a marble stair that led down to the bathroom. The floor was slippery and we had to be careful. The room wasn't exactly clean but the sheets were, and really that was all I cared about.

We took a walk around and realized how many tourists were here in Krabi. There was no vacancy anywhere. We found a nice restaurant around the corner from where we stayed. We had an early night and slept well.

In the morning there was a truck that went from hotel to hotel picking up tourists that were taking the passenger ferry, a large boat going to the islands. The truck was absolutely stuffed full with tourists and on top of the truck was everyone's luggage plus my wheelchair with one large wheel hanging precariously over the ledge. Thankfully we didn't have far to go.

We reached the dock and we all poured out of the truck. We could see the ferry in the distance. The boat didn't look that large but it had been stuffed tighter with tourists than a vacuum-packed bag. I was sure that if we were back at home, that amount of people on a boat of that size would have been highly illegal. The boat disgorged the multitude.

Finally, it was our turn to walk up the ramp and find a seat. Bernie had pushed our way towards the front. I was the only person in a wheelchair, but people are people and some shoved their way in front of us.

Bernie seated us under the canopy which covered half of the boat. The ten life vests were located within reach — obviously not enough for the seventy or so people on board.

Oh well, I tried to reassure myself, I just wouldn't think of the possible negative events that could very well happen. I was remembering our train trip from Bangkok when the train brakes were put back together and there were left over pieces on the ground. I just closed my eyes and hoped it wasn't a good day for the boat to capsize or for us to drown.

The boat slowed down at one point, then stopped. What was going on? There was a small island on the way to the much larger Koh Lanta where we were headed. Four small wooden motorized boats were approaching. Then we watched as half a dozen people threw their small backpacks into the small boats and jumped into the beautiful clear water of the Andaman Sea and were assisted into the boats. We were told they were headed for the very small island we saw from the ferry. If we ever went back that way again I'd be jumping in the water and swimming to that beautiful white powdery beach. There wasn't any electricity there; everything was run on generators just like many rural areas of Thailand or outlying Islands. That was fine by me. We had been to too many places in our travels where it was difficult to find Wi-Fi except at an internet bar. On our trip to

Placencia, Belize, the country held "black outs" every evening. We read by candlelight. It was so peaceful and romantic reading and listening to the waves roll ashore. In our crazy, busy, technology-obsessed world most places seem too noisy and it grates on my brain.

The boat ride took two hours and we enjoyed the sea splashing into our faces. Finally, we arrived in another paradise: long, white, sandy beaches and sparkling clear aqua water. This was the part of our Thailand trip I had been waiting for. I loved beautiful sunny beaches with soft white sand like powder and clear, warm water. Oh yes, and palm trees and coconuts.

CHAPTER 24

Paradise

Travelling is all the education you need
— *KL I*

We found our bungalow at a small resort of inexpensive cement bungalows with thatched roofs and an outdoor shower. We were in a bungalow fairly close to the beach but also right beside the restaurant with its generator running from early morning to ten or eleven at night. We stayed close to the resort that evening, had a cold beer on the restaurant patio, took a nap, and then ate dinner there also. We were tired from our adventures of the past two weeks and we both wanted to be beach sloths.

We sat on the beach for a couple of days; well I did, and Bernie was always under a tree on his hammock, somewhere out of the direct sun. He's smart but I am not. I loooove the sunshine. It soothes me.

The next day we had a so-so breakfast at our resort's outdoor restaurant then headed for a walk into town. We found out there was going to be a special festival that night, the lighting of the lanterns, or Loi Krathong, in Old Lanta Town, celebrated annually on the full moon in November.

I loved it when we got away from the touristy things of the countries we visited. Bernie arranged for a ride to take us there and back. The driver didn't speak very much English so we were hoping we wouldn't get stranded there without a way home. Sometimes we had to throw caution to the wind and go with our gut feeling. We got back to our bungalow early in the afternoon. We changed into our bathing suits and I headed to the beach while Bernie hung up his hammock in the shade.

I ventured into the water a few times. It was warm and the waves were perfect for body surfing. I gave up after a few tries; I ended up either getting knocked over or swept back up onto the beach with my bathing suit full of sand. The tide was in but over the next week and a half we saw how far out the tide retreated and we would stick me in the wheelchair and go "off roading" over the bumpy wet sand. I loved it.

After our afternoon rest and a shower we ventured back into town for dinner. The food was only so-so. We had had such delicious food up north and on Khaosan Road in Bangkok that this was a huge disappointment. However, soon we would be meeting up with our driver in town and we were excited about seeing the lantern festival.

The ride there and back to Old Lanta Town was an adventure on its own. We were picked up in a *songthaew*, a covered pick-up truck with wooden benches. Some of the larger trucks could take up to forty people seated in the truck and standing on a platform at the back. Thankfully, we were not in one of those; the ride wasn't comfortable at all even so.

The roads were very bumpy and it seemed there were no shock absorbers at all. The driver picked up several Thai people, mostly men, along the way. We were the only Caucasian tourists but again we felt very comfortable. This was an important event for the locals. Loi Krathong was celebrated throughout Thailand. Families and friends gathered at the sea, rivers, and canals to pay respect to the water spirits, Buddha, and their elders, and also to symbolically float away their troubles. Wishes were made for the year to come.

It was a beautiful festival of lights. People made their own small boats out of light wood, a coconut shell, or a banana leaf. The boats were decorated with lit candles and flowers, and people put various small items onboard that had significance to them. Some were very elaborate.

It was good to get out of the *songthaew* — our behinds were sore from all the potholes along the way. We had been taken to a large field where the main festival for Koh Lanta was held. We did see a few other Caucasian travellers wandering around. There was a beauty pageant on a stage and other entertainment here and there; we wandered around checking out the people and the many food vendors: so many choices of delicious-smelling food. They even had sweet roll-up pancakes that were very yummy. I probably had six. I had to fatten up my behind for the bumpy ride back to our beach house.

We saw that we could purchase already-made boats with flowers and other decorations and candles. We bought one to share. It was exciting taking part in a yearly traditional festival we had previously had no idea we would be a part of.

The sun was finally fully down and the sky was alight with the full moon. Most of the people at the festival headed down to the water to light their boats and send them to be carried off over the water, hoping their wishes would come true for the next year.

The scene was simply magnificent. Hundreds of small floating platforms or tiny boat-shaped hand-made vessels were released into the sea. We lit our candles on top of our little float, said our thanks, and thought of family. It was one of the most beautiful scenes I've seen. Tranquil, sparkling, satisfying, amazing, completely mesmerizing. Peaceful.

The *songthaew* was right where we expected it to be at the end of the evening. We were exhausted and I really don't remember the ride being nearly as rough back to Koh Lanta as on the way to Old Lanta Town.

I made a big error in judgment the next morning, agreeing to have a massage by a woman on the beach. I was in so much pain at one point I couldn't speak. I finally yelled out when she — not a small lady — stood on my upper legs. Was she trying to kill me? I had heard of these painful Thai massages but this was worse than I could imagine. She was so sure she could help me after seeing me in the wheelchair. I should not have listened. It was brutal.

After lunch and a rest I actually did feel better so we ventured down the street to where scooters were rented. The scooter seat was narrow enough that my five-foot-nothing body with short legs could fit comfortably. It sure beat getting around in the wheelchair. It was freedom for me and for Bernie; he didn't have to push me everywhere.

We didn't get too far that day, just into the main village of Saladan to look around to see where we might do some touristy shopping. We also stopped at a restaurant overlooking the water and had a beer: nice and cold and refreshing, served in a freezer-chilled glass.

I was starting to have a lot of pain. I think the massage after-effects were setting in. I told myself I would never do that again.

We rested for a long time then went to the restaurant next door, the one with the loud generator. The food was delicious. I nearly always had fish of some sort, and Bernie usually had chicken. My fish was fresh caught that day and I could choose the fish from a large covered tray with ice, for the cook to make for me.

There were several beach dogs around the restaurants in the evening. They were nice-looking dogs: well kept, and well-fed, anyway. One small labrador retriever mix came and lay down on my feet under our table — just like that. I missed our poochie at home.

I had several bruises popping up here and there where the crazy masseuse who spoke no English had done her damage. Ouch.

We had a good sleep. The next day we got up, had breakfast, got our bathing suits on, lay on the beach and read books, went swimming ... Sometimes life is as simple as that. Perfect.

We rented a scooter again and travelled around Koh Lanta for a three-hour tour.

About halfway around we came upon a very steep dirt road just around a corner with many potholes. Half-way up this steep hill the tires started spinning and couldn't get a grip on the dirt. We started rolling backwards. I was terrified we'd go over the side, which was very steep, so I hopped off and Bernie tried to get himself and the scooter up the hill. He did, but the road looked like it went up a long way and we didn't know where it might lead to, so we turned around.

After dinner we went to the open-air restaurant where we were staying, to take pictures of the sunset. We met a woman from Australia taking photos also. She had such a great sense of humour we laughed and chatted with her for a long time.

When I went to bed that evening my chest felt tight. I had been feeling weak and wiped out, however that didn't stop me from sitting on the beach or jumping on the back of our small motorcycle and touring around the areas we hadn't yet seen. I thought my chest tightness might be from my asthma as I had forgotten to take my inhaler more than once while we had been up north. Every morning and evening my chest felt worse and now my throat was red and very sore. Bernie convinced me to start the antibiotics we had brought along. Thankfully, my sore throat went away and my chest was not nearly as congested after I took the round of antibiotics. I did feel much better, for a day or so anyway.

We had dinner with the young woman from Australia. The next day she was going to be certified for ocean diving. She was nervous but we reassured her and yes, she passed.

The day after, we rented another motorbike; this one was very comfortable, unlike the one we had the day before. We were going exploring again. I took many photos while sitting on the back of the small motorbike and they all turned out beautifully.

We were headed to a natural habitat for monkeys but first we decided to go to the sea gypsy village where the Thai sea gypsies lived — either on boats or in three-sided shacks built from wood, with a tin or wooden roof, on stilts close to the water.

There was a deadly tsunami that occurred three years before our trip. It hit Thailand's Andaman sea coast hard, but none of the sea gypsies perished. They lived on the water, and knew its rhythm from hundreds of years of knowledge passed down from the elders. They read the sea that day and went out past the waves or to high land. Not one of the sea gypsies died, but 230,000 others did up the coast, and many villages were wiped out.

We slowly puttered around the small village, everyone waving hello to us. There was one three-sided shack where three or four women were watching a large TV. One woman was holding her baby who kept trying to scurry away. The TV stretched from one side of the shack to the other. I was so mind-boggled trying to wrap my head around the fact that these people had almost nothing, but had a huge TV. Maybe it was the only one in the village for all to use. There were a few small houses and a small store nearby; they may have had TVs too. I don't know.

As we carried along down the road away from the village, we could see that the government had been building some row houses out of concrete, painted yellow with brown trim. Bernie remarked that modernization may be the sea gypsy's demise. These people never integrated into Thailand and remain a "tribe" apart. They had their own dialect and traditions.

We had asked for directions to the area where we could see monkeys in the wild. Firstly we were told to find the "monkey school" to arrange for a guide from there to take us in a songthaew to view the monkey in the wild.

It took a lot longer than we were told to get to the monkey school. A monkey school? That's exactly what it was. We were very disappointed, as we didn't want to see tamed monkeys who had been taught to play basketball or otherwise clipped to a chain. Who knows, maybe the monkeys liked playing basketball, but I was sure that given a choice they would rather be free. We received directions to carry on a dirt side road to our destination where our guide and Songthaew would take us to see the wild monkeys near along the waterway.

We carried on down the long bumpy road and came upon a resort, of sorts. There were tree houses and a few made out of wood that looked like boats in a tree. What a hoot. After looking around we found a beautiful teak bar. How did tourists find these little hideaways? Just like we did I guess, roaming around away from the heavy tourist areas.

We bought some water; I was feeling very dehydrated and in pain. I took some pain medication and decided I could carry on. I really wanted to see the monkeys in the wild.

We had gone down this road too far. The woman at the bar gave us directions and considering it was on our way back to our bungalow we decided to go and see it even though we were both tired.

Finally, we found the correct road. We parked the bike and then had to walk down a very rickety boardwalk, missing rungs here and there, with water below us. We noticed some fish, well we thought they were fish as they looked like fish, fins and all, but these ones also had legs. *Ok*, I thought, *now I have seen everything.* I had to shake my head a few times to make sure I was seeing what I was seeing. At the end of the boardwalk was a wooden longboat with a driver waiting for us who spoke no English but had a lot of fruit in the boat. Pineapple, bananas, mango, and watermelon.

We had to climb down five rungs to get into the boat. It was a little dicey with my wonky balance but I managed to get into the narrow longboat and not to fall into the water with the prehistoric-looking short-legged fish.

After some time cruising up the channel we saw a lot of mangroves and many birds of different species. We came to a stop near the bank of the water and spotted a few monkeys. We took turns tossing fruit onto the banks of the river. Suddenly there were monkeys flying out of the trees, dozens of them, big and small, boys, girls, mommies and daddies. One was a big dude who didn't like to share and would push the smaller ones out of the way from a prime piece of pineapple. At last one of the young monkeys caught a piece of fruit and quickly ran away to protect his find. It was like watching a bunch of unruly toddlers and a bully.

All in all it was an incredible day, but I knew I'd be sore in the morning, and I was.

A couple of days later we explored Koh Lanta Noi, (Small Island). This part of Koh Lanta was government-owned and immaculately kept. We had to take a short ferry ride to get there from Koh Lanta Yai (Large Island). There were two large undeveloped beaches on Lanta Noi and the air was sweet: no diesel fuel or other pollution here.

Koh Lanta Noi was peaceful, quiet. No tourist resorts, loud bars or generators on this beach.

There were interesting rubber plantations and some Muslim fishing villages. Most of Koh Lanta is Muslim, however not as strict as in some countries. There is alcohol available and tourists don't need to cover up when outdoors. People here lived a simple life and often were poor from the look of some of the houses. Many just looked like broken-down huts. But the government road was newly paved and as we got closer to the ferry we saw a large government health care building, not a hospital. There were other government buildings and nearby were much nicer houses than we had seen on the rest of the island, where it seemed the government workers lived.

On both big and small Koh Lanta there were rubber plantations, fields of rubber trees tapped for the dripping rubber direct from the tree. It was similar to Eastern Canada where maple trees are tapped in the spring for the famous Canadian maple syrup.

We were running out of gas in our scooter so we purchased some from a woman with a small baby in a small house that had a large drum of gasoline out front.

A *songthaew* driver was there, filling up large plastic bags with gasoline — soda pop was also sold in plastic bags. Don't get the two mixed up! Health and safety standards simply didn't exist in some parts of Thailand, most parts of Thailand. But we didn't live there and our standards were based on knowledge in North America. There were, however, many tsunami warning signs very visible around this "gas station" and main Koh Lanta, directing travellers to higher ground. What I had learned on this trip so far was to expect the unexpected — as in life.

We returned to Koh Lanta Yai on the same stinky, almost broken-down ferry we had taken earlier to get here. The wires were badly frayed and there were only four lifejackets visible anywhere, for dozens of people.

We also learned about the way of life for many in the restaurants. We got to know a couple of sweet waitresses at our favourite restaurant with the loud generator beside our bungalow. They told us they worked seven days a week for twelve to fourteen hours, sometimes with not much of a break between breakfast, lunch, and dinner. I was sure their pay was low, we always tipped well. Most of the waiters and waitresses came from up north to work during the busy tourist months on the beaches. They left their families behind and sent them money. The parents of our foster girl also travelled south to obtain work when not sowing or harvesting.

Paradise for us, not so much for native Thais.

Every evening on the beach, near one or another beach restaurant, there were fire dancers giving everyone a show.

We usually sat on the patio area of our resort restaurant watching the sun set.

Sometime around six every evening we watched a Swedish stroller parade. Many Swedes travelled here on holidays and some lived here. In the evening the parents would push their young ones in a stroller, one after another, a couple of them side by side, with other children tagging along, and the beach dogs too. It really was like a parade of beautiful blonde women and children and dogs.

A gecko had moved into our bungalow and would scurry up and across the walls. It was a little unnerving at times. I was concerned he/she might fall off the wall when we were sleeping. Of course that never happened and we considered the gecko our guest. I kept saying *It isn't a snake,* that's all I cared about. Some friends of ours moved to Thailand and later sent us a picture of the humongous snake that moved into their house. No thank you. Nope and no way, not ever. Sorry snakes, don't take it personally.

It was our last day there and I was glad. I felt like I'd been hit by a truck. My head hurt and my sore throat and laryngitis kept coming back. I had taken the full week of antibiotics and I felt improved for a few days but now it felt like pneumonia. My cough was terrifying. I couldn't seem to catch my breath. Oh well, we would be home in a couple of days and I would rather have seen my own doctor. We had met a couple sitting on the beach visiting from Great Britain. She was a registered nurse like me, and she had been to the hospital for an infection. She was appalled at the state of affairs at this hospital. The antibiotics were outdated, but that was all they had, and same with the intravenous fluids. I wasn't keen on going to that hospital. I might very well turn out worse than before I had gone in.

The weather on our second to last day had been cloudy. We had a storm blow through the day before and we got caught in the torrential downpour and sought shelter under some palm trees with giant leaves. There was another person, a businessman, who also got caught in the downpour. We were all soaked including my wheelchair but the sun came out again and it must have been nearly 40 degrees Celsius.

The only day Bernie went into the water was on our last day, when the waves were high and the water murky when it was normally a beautiful turquoise. That was the kind of guy he was and he had fun riding the waves. I swam one more time. I felt horrible, my whole body ached, and I was sure I had a fever. I was looking forward to sleeping in my own bed and not under mosquito netting.

That evening we watched the sunset in Koh Lanta for the last time on this trip. There were about thirty boats visible on the horizon and after it got dark we could see the lights shining in the water. They were catching squid by shining lights into the water which brought the curious creatures to the surface to be caught.

We got up, had a not-so-good breakfast at the resort's outdoor restaurant and waited for the bus/van to take us back to Krabi, then a plane to Bangkok, and a stopover in Taiwan.

I was doing my best not to cough in the van. I knew if I started it would be hard to quit. I wasn't the only one coughing; a man behind me was coughing badly. I had never meditated so deeply in order to keep myself calm and not cough.

Our trip to Taiwan was fairly uneventful but I did get worried when we had to walk by a temperature reader. I crossed my fingers because I was sure mine was high. But it wasn't. I also didn't realize at the time that I may have been contagious. I was hoping not. I had been sick for almost three weeks and I thought the contagion stage had passed. I just wanted to get home.

CHAPTER 25

Hippocratic Oath

What doesn't kill you makes you stronger.
— Friedrich Nietzsche, you are wrong!

It was a long journey home with a stopover for several hours in Taiwan late in the evening. We had booked a room in the first class lounge that we were allowed to use as we had flown business class. It was perfect; we snoozed for a few hours, had a shower, caught the plane very early the next morning, and back home we went. I only coughed a couple of times into my carry-on blanket and hopefully didn't share my germs. I didn't feel great but nor did I feel really as sick as I had been.

By the time we got home Bernie was coughing. After a few days he was coughing badly. One evening he was coughing so hard he couldn't catch his breath. Nothing seemed to help and we finally had to call the emergency number and the paramedics arrived. I followed the ambulance to the hospital. It turned out we both had pertussis (aka whooping cough). It never even occurred to me that it could be what was considered a childhood disease which had been eradicated, or so I thought. Before our trip we had attended a travel clinic to make sure we had all of the vaccines/immunizations required, plus antibiotics, which probably helped me a lot. Pertussis is a bacterial infection and is highly contagious. Both Bernie and I had had all of our juvenile vaccinations and we thought we were still protected from whooping cough. The incidence of pertussis in North America is very, very low — almost unheard of — like measles and mumps, which are preventable as long as children get their vaccines in a timely manner. Yes, some children still get these diseases as vaccine protection is never 100 percent. My daughter had both types of measles and contracted pneumonia with one type. I am a firm believer in vaccinations but these infections can still occur. After thinking back upon our trip I remembered vividly the older Swede walking down the steps of the bleachers at the elephant festival, coughing like he was about to expire and the many people he would have infected that day. Who knew where he may have contracted pertussis?

It took awhile to completely mend but we did. I still had to use the wheelchair on most outings but preferred to take my walker. The wheelchair tires had to be replaced as they had melted down to the rim. Yes, we had burned rubber, but wheelchair wheels can be replaced. After all the activity we did in Thailand I had been so sure I would be much stronger, but that was definitely not the case. Had I burned out too?

Back home my family doctors (two left after one year of practice each) moved out of the province and were replaced by another young woman who actually understood chronic pain and was aghast at the amount of narcotics that were going into my five-foot, 100 pound body every day.

Several years later I found out through DNA testing that I was an ultra-rapid metabolizer of most medications. For example, opioids such as regular morphine have a half-life of two to four hours. That meant that half of the drug was eliminated in that time. But with me the clearance rate was much faster, not giving me the full benefit of the medication. No wonder I was in pain if the heavy duty opioids had been clearing my system so fast. However, in the year 2022 we still don't have "personalized medicine". One day we will, but until then we are all treated the same whether we are six feet tall and 200 pounds or five feet tall and 100 pounds. Some people have high metabolism, some have low. Some people are opioid naive; some have been off and on some type of opioid for years. Even low dose opioids count. Each person may metabolize drugs in a slightly different way; our brains don't function the same way as everyone else's. However, long-term use of opioids can have other detrimental effects whether they are metabolized normally or not.

During those years there was an unfortunate "misunderstanding" of a clinical report on opioids perpetuated by Big Pharma. It was believed opioids were not addictive for those with chronic pain. That turned out to be an incorrect interpretation of how opioids actually worked and caused huge problems with addiction and tolerance.

The sentence that Big Pharma grabbed onto was taken out of context. However, this statement, even though taken out of context, was in a major medical journal, *The Lancet*, and had been cited over six hundred times, thus convincing physicians that opioids were not addictive for people with chronic pain. Nobody, it seemed, read the full article on opioids and addiction.

There had been only a few days in my life, for as long as I could remember, when I had zero pain. I couldn't believe the difference being pain-free, or almost; but after a bit of time the dosage of fentanyl kept getting higher and higher while I felt a lot worse with horrible pain — at times so bad I would pass out.

A new family practice doctor recognized something was terribly wrong and sent me to an addiction specialist. I was reluctant to go to a psychiatrist who specialized in addiction. I was sure I'd be brushed off again as having depression and being a hypochondriac with too many symptoms to be true. I was getting very tired of explaining myself to doctors who did not believe me. Plus I wasn't addicted to opioids: *I'm a stronger person than that!! I'm an RN; I would know if I was addicted.* But I was tired of taking all those opioids and I wanted to get off them.

This doctor turned out to be very helpful and very knowledgeable. He weaned me off all the opioids, a slow and painful process. I hadn't realized I was addicted. I couldn't see myself anymore.

Addiction was a lonely hell. Big Pharma grew addicts like weeds. I was so lucky to have been sent to this addiction specialist/psychiatrist. Without him, and my new family doctor I just might have overdosed or ended up buying street drugs. I worry about all the others that had been put on opioids in the nineties and even up until just a few years ago. The majority may not realize they are addicted or may have developed tolerance. Part of the problem starting opioids is that most, if not all, people will develop tolerance at some point, some quicker than others. Tolerance can happen in as little as one month on opioids.

Tolerance occurs when all the opioids receptors (mu receptors) in the brain get plugged with opioids and the medication is not metabolized and becomes useless over time. That's a simplistic way of looking at tolerance. Basically, the brain changes the way it processes opioids and causes desensitization. Opioids also interfere with the amount of dopamine released. Dopamine is the pleasure-inducing neurotransmitter. Initially, opioids enhance dopamine release but as time goes by, with chronic opioid use the dopamine decreases, causing cravings for increased opioids.

Rotating opioids helps, but just a little; no matter what opioid is used they bind to mu receptors in the brain, spinal cord, and stomach — and when those receptors change after long-term use, the opioid becomes useless as it passes through the system unconverted.

Whether someone is a housewife, a student, a lawyer, a doctor, or any other person who ever takes an opioid, five percent will become addicted, according to the New Canadian Opioid Guidelines (McMaster University, Ontario, 2017) This is not just a street person's disease. It often starts at home with the first opioid prescription. Five percent of Canadians equals nearly two million people who are addicts, and they are definitely not all residing on the streets or stealing, but they are a big safety concern — to themselves and others.

You can imagine my horror at the realization I was addicted to morphine. I was able to get off the fentanyl without any problem but part of getting off opioids involved a weaning process whereby I was put on liquid morphine toward the end of the rehab. I accidentally spilled about a half teaspoon of morphine on the kitchen counter when I was trying to dose each amount into 3cc syringes. That's when I realized what addiction entailed. I was feeling horrified and humiliated when I was so desperate not to waste any amount of morphine I actually licked it off the counter and I would have licked it off the floor if necessary. It had a grip on me; it was making me crazy.

I asked the pharmacy if I could get my prescription a day early due to the spill. Very reluctantly and with several frowns, multiple questions and lectures in front of others, they filled the next bottle of liquid morphine. I wanted to fall down and cry. I had gone to that pharmacy for twenty years. They knew me well, but still the shame was palpable. I felt like screaming at them that it wasn't my fault. A highly trained head of pharmacology at a major university started me on that whack of opioids including fentanyl. It's NOT my fucking fault!

I was not a street addict, I was not begging on the street for money for drugs, I didn't steal, and I had a college degree. *I'm a good person! Help me please!* I wanted to die right there and then.

I could barely wait until my next dose. I was glued to the clock in anticipation. Addiction can happen to anyone. I was mortified.

I also craved sweets which became worse towards the end of rehab. I gobbled down doughnuts and home-baked goodies trying to find a sugar high. The dopamine in my brain that controlled reward and pleasure was screaming at me to feed it, and sugar helped. I could be a stubborn person and there was no way I would be beaten at this trial of life. There was no way I ever wanted to go through the rehab experience again. I won. Yes, I gained a lot of weight but it came off quickly and unfortunately my weight kept going down over a couple of years until I weighed eighty-three pounds. My weight, which had been steady for many years, was yo-yoing and I didn't like it. I had to change my wardrobe several times over the years.

Another issue that can develop and did for me, is long term use of opioids can cause allodynia where even light touch can cause pain. Hyperalgesia, similar to allodynia, has been related to chronic opioid use and can damage nerves or cause chemical changes that increase the sensation of pain. That was me all over. There had been times I couldn't scratch my back or arm without feeling like I've set fire to my skin. I felt horrible when Bernie tried to cuddle with me and I was pleading with him to not touch me. This went on for years.

I got off the opioids. It was a horrible time but I did it. I wouldn't wish anyone to have to go through rehab to stop long-term opioid use. My recommendation is just don't start taking them in the first place. Easy to say, but going on opioids without trials of other medications should not be the first choice, not even Tylenol 3. Codeine is an opioid.

There are also psychological effects for people in pain; going on opioids shows others in their lives that they are truly in terrible pain. Some people — many people — end up with damaged relationships, or family members who think they are lying or lazy because they may not to be able to see their medical condition. There's no way to test how much chronic pain one endures day after day.

CHAPTER 26

Planning our next trip

Wherever you go becomes a part of you somehow.
— Anita Desai

We had loved our journey to Thailand so much we started to plan our next trip.

We continued taking Thai lessons every week from our tutor and were very pleased with the number of words we knew. We hoped our next visit would be even better, being able to communicate a wee bit more in Thai.

I had fallen in love with Thailand and its people who were so kind and helpful, but children in the poor rural areas needed a proper education to better help their families and communities. Before we knew it we decided to start our own charity raising money to help buy school products for the rest of the schools in that region.

It was a great idea, or so we thought at the time. We began filling out all the government forms to apply for a charity designation. It took months and months to do. Finding people to be on the required board wasn't easy but we did it. On and on we went. It was a great learning experience. I made a lot of mistakes and was getting frustrated and overwhelmed by the process. Bernie was still working full-time so I puttered along setting up the charity and planning our next trip.

Meanwhile, I gave up going for treatment after treatment: physiotherapy, massage therapy, acupuncture, and so many more. I vowed to continue each therapy for a minimum of six visits or six weeks. Not one therapy helped me to feel stronger. Most made me feel worse. It was an exhausting existence. The pain was horrible, my energy depleted, yet nobody seemed to know what was wrong with me except now my family doctor at least finally agreed with the fibromyalgia diagnosis

A year and a half went by very fast, as time seems to do. It's absolutely true that the older one gets the faster time goes by. I get whiplash trying to keep up.

It was time to return to Thailand, complete with our newly-formed charity *Thais that Bind* and the hope of adding some Thai people to our charity with the aim of raising money to provide proper school supplies at least in the Isaan area. One half-piece of chalk for the teacher and half a pencil for each child was ridiculous. There were no — or very few — textbooks or writing papers. It was difficult to see how any student could properly learn in school. Public schools were all free until grade twelve, which was great, but there were so few educational tools to actually teach properly.

Bernie and I decided we could use one of the nurses we met on our first trip as a middleman, so to speak. Her husband was a teacher in Sisaket near where our foster daughter and family lived.

We sent 500 Canadian dollars to her bank, which was a challenge and a half. Banking was not done online in Thailand then and converting Canadian dollars to Thai *baht* seemed to be a difficult challenge at my bank. It finally got sent. The money was for the nurse to buy 500 dollars of school items for our foster girl's school. The nurse and her helpers did an excellent job and sent us many pictures. We were overjoyed that a relatively small amount of money could do so much.

CHAPTER 27

Thailand Adventure #2

The chief danger in life is that you may take too many precautions.

— Alfred Adler

This time we journeyed to Thailand in the spring. We flew to Taiwan on the wonderful Singapore Airlines and had a few hours layover, but not enough time to book a room in the first-class lounge this trip.

Bangkok again; I didn't feel nearly as intimidated as our first trip. We stayed in a different hotel, not nearly as nice as the first time but still nice.

Bangkok was still a dirty, polluted and over-crowded city but it did have its attractions.

The first time we went to Thailand Bernie didn't sleep much on the plane and after our arrival in Bangkok he probably slept twelve hours. This time it was me. I didn't have any earplugs and I hardly slept at all on the plane but I sure crashed after our arrival in Bangkok. I ended up sleeping eighteen hours with a break after twelve hours for some food. Both of us missed lunch and dinner but by the day after that we felt much better, more acclimatized.

We went for a long walk around the area where we were staying. I wasn't nearly as intimidated; I knew what to expect, I hoped.

We were to meet up with our Thai language teacher's friends for dinner that evening. We were very excited to meet his friends. We waited just a short time in the hotel lobby and the two nurses, Manee and Nok, arrived to take us to the restaurant to meet up with one of the nurses' husband, the doctor. He was an orthopedic specialist and worked in the International Hospital in Bangkok.

The two women had taken their four-year nursing program together. One nurse lived with her husband, the doctor, in Bangkok. The other nurse lived with her husband, Somchai, in Sisaket, not too far from our foster family's village. We were taking the train later that night to Sisaket and Somchai was going to meet us in the morning at the train station to take us to our hotel.

It took us over an hour to get to the restaurant. It was rush hour and a fifteen minute drive turned out to be very long. We finally found a parking lot with a spot left. It was quite a walk to the restaurant, for me anyway. I had just brought my cane; the women had thought they would be able to park close. I probably needed a stretch anyway.

At the restaurant we met the doctor and some of the nurses' friends. Our dinner was delicious. I felt I lost and felt I had forgotten all the Thai words we had learned, but between the doctor, who spoke some English, and us, with our very beginner-level Thai, we all managed to have a great time.

We were driven to the train station afterwards. Again we had a smaller bag to travel northeast and we left the wheelchair at the luggage storage at our hotel. We had made the trip once before so it was easier to judge if I would need the wheelchair or not. I would do fine without it. It would be so much easier to get on and off the train.

This time our train left late and managed to get behind even more along the way. We ended up arriving two hours past the stated arrival time. I was very concerned because we had no way of contacting Somchai, who was to meet us at the train station in the morning.

The train ride was almost the same experience as I had the last time. I think I flooded the bathroom floor trying to clean the urine down the drain. Another totally embarrassing and humbling experience. That time I wore sandals that were much easier to clean than the running shoes I had worn on the first trip.

Somchai didn't seem concerned about our late arrival. He was a teacher and we found out later how he was able to take time off to wait and retrieve us from the train station. We went to a nearby restaurant and had a delicious breakfast. Bernie and I were exhausted, so with apologies to Somchai, we went to our hotel for a rest.

Later we were picked up by Somchai and his twins, a boy and girl aged eight — Nok, his wife was working. We went to a restaurant where we sat Japanese-style with cushions on the floor around a rectangular table; we ate everything they ordered. Sometimes, it's best not to know exactly what is in the food served.

It was dark by the time we finished and were dropped off back at our hotel. It wasn't really late but the sun had set around seven. The kids in the back of the station wagon had fallen asleep. Our very amiable Plan Thai volunteer translator and the same volunteer driver picked us up at nine in the morning at our hotel. I was never an early riser but we had to meet our foster girl and family by a certain time so the kids could go back to school and the adults to work in the fields.

We were about forty-five minutes away from the town Huay Thap Than, and then another fifteen minutes drive on a very bumpy, dusty road to the small rural village where our foster girl lived.

We stopped in Huay Thap Than, as we did on the first visit to the small village, to buy supplies for lunch and gifts for the school. We knew we weren't supposed to buy anything for the family as outlined on our do's and don'ts from the charity, but how could we say no, especially when we seemed like very wealthy people from North America. So we watched as the translator started stuffing baskets with toothbrushes, soap, all kinds of this and that, small items that were needed by the children, and some for the adults. Then the chicken and fish were plunked in the basket. We were trying politely to assess how much had gone in the baskets but it all came to a small amount when we did the *baht* to Canadian dollar exchange. We finally arrived at the village and there were many more people here to greet us than the first trip.

Grandma and grandpa were still alive, although the first time we met them they were so wrinkled and small I thought they were ready for the grave. There were mom and dad, older aunties, younger aunties, cousins, a representative from our charity, the village administrator, our driver, and translator all sitting or standing under the house in the shade.

There was food galore. It really was a feast and we realized we had only contributed a small amount. A couple of young women volunteers from the charity in Thailand kept bringing us coconut water directly from the coconut as they had on our first visit. We were exploding with fluids but apparently we were dehydrated as we didn't need to urinate for several hours.

Before we ate they brought us precious water to rinse our hands. Both of us felt humbled and remembered that we had asked on the first visit to wash our hands. Water was always extremely scarce and as Canadians we took water for granted. We weren't immune to the germs here and knew we'd be eating lunch with our hands again. But water was a precious commodity and everyone present for lunch would be eating with their hands so it really made no difference.

We waited for somebody to start eating or pass the food around. Nobody moved, so Bernie and I finally started. This time we used the few spoons available to take some food from the bowls and we put the spoon back on the table or in the serving bowl. We had seen before how the others had taken some sticky rice, rolled it into a small ball, and then used it as a scoop to take food from the other bowls. We were finally "getting it".

Everyone was much more relaxed this visit. Bernie kept them laughing with our attempts to speak Thai. He wasn't shy talking but would forget words and that's where I came in, as my word recall was pretty good. We just loved the acceptance.

Time went by too fast and our foster girl had to return to school. Her dad was taking her on the back of his motorcycle/dirt bike. To our enormous delight she gave us a hug before she jumped on the bike behind her dad and drove away. What a sweet girl. That hug really made this trip special.

We were taken on a tour of the village to see all the new developments since the last time we visited, including a small warehouse where women could work and raise money by sewing tourist novelties such as cloth purses. They were able to work part-time and choose their hours. They also had a day-care so the women could work without worrying about their babies.

Another development was the huge, blue, water cistern. So that's where they got the water for us to wash our hands. Another change was the construction of more homes in the village. These new houses were made from cement and not raised high like the wooden dwellings were. A nice new house was being built for the village mayor, or some sort of dignitary.

On our walk-about through the very small village we saw all kinds of dwellings including rusted tin shacks, lean-tos, and one house with a skinny cow in the front of a house. It looked ready to fall over — the cow and the house.

We had hoped to visit the local school again but they were doing important exams and we would be disturbing the whole school.

We were driven back to our hotel by the charity's driver and our interpreter. We immediately lay down on the bed, we were very exhausted. We woke up three hours later for dinner in our room, then went back to bed again; we finally fell back to sleep at one in the morning; we had to get up early the next morning.

Back home before we left for Thailand I tried to get some documentation of how the 500 dollars had been spent on supplies. We never did receive the certificate or receipts for the money we had sent. We received pictures and we saw everything that was bought for the kids at our foster girl's school but we needed an itemized list in order to determine how much money should be raised to help each child, not just at this school, but others across Isaan. At the time I hadn't realized how busy Nok was and now I felt bad about asking for her help. She had helped us so much and in my haste and anxiety with my medical condition — plus the fact we didn't speak the same language — I felt I had asked too much. She was not only a registered nurse but also a nursing practitioner. She was doing most of what doctors do, but she was also studying for her bar exam. She had spent some time in France for part of her education and spoke Thai and French. What an intelligent, wonderful, woman and family. We'll always be grateful for their help and putting up with us.

Sonchai was a teacher at the local school. We could hardly believe our good fortune at having met this couple through our Thai language teacher in Vancouver, to be able to stay with them and experience Thai life. Sonchai was Vietnamese but was raised in France. He spoke six languages including English and taught Mandarin in the local school. Good, we thought, great contact for our charity. This was getting exciting; thoughts of our charity helping the schools in this part of Thailand were becoming real.

On this visit to Sisaket, Sonchai and Nok had set up a meeting with a very important man in the region who wanted to meet us and talk about our charity *Thais That Bind*, and work on developing a plan. This was beyond our wildest dreams, or at least mine.

It was a good thing we would be meeting the VIP man who ran the stationery store — the biggest school and stationery supplier in the region; he also had a high elected position in the government of the province. We had a lot of questions about how our charity could work in the Isaan area. We were excited to meet this man as he would be a key factor in getting supplies to all the schools in the region. We would start with two or three schools and proceed from there.

Sonchai called us at 7:15 the next morning. As I have mentioned, I am not a morning person but we had to get up because we had been invited to stay at our new friend's home, and first we were going on a tour around Sisaket. We saw many interesting *wats* including one made completely out of bottles — all kinds of pop and beer bottles, the old fashioned kind. It was so unique and fun to see the sun shine through the green and brown glass.

After lunch we picked up Nok and the children to go for a walk in the park. It was a beautiful green park with lots of room to wander. Families were having picnics. We crossed a wooden bridge over churning, bubbly water. What in the world was going on? It looked like a scene from some horror movie. The small river was absolutely full with catfish — very large catfish that crashed and pummeled each other which made the water appear as if it were boiling. I can't say I was all excited about seeing these ugly, black, google-eyed monsters but I did take a lot of pictures.

By the time our day was done I was completely worn out. The past two days I had managed to walk around everywhere with my cane. My legs were very painful but I was happy. Not many people got a chance like this, experiencing life in a foreign, developing country.

Our friend's house was in a residential area, quiet except for a yappy little dog next door that never seemed to quit barking, day or night. Their house was two-storied white stucco, with a carport. The houses in this neighbourhood were of different styles and sizes, and not all made from the same materials.

The kitchen was on the main floor. It was big compared to the other rooms in the house. There's nothing like a big kitchen to welcome people. We felt right at home. The main floor also had two bedrooms and a bathroom which was all tile and the tub was on a platform. Fancy.

Their guest bedroom was upstairs beside the small TV room. The bedroom was small and had a twin-size bed. Bernie is six feet tall with long arms and legs; I'm only five feet tall and don't weigh much over one hundred pounds so you can imagine how our night went. At the same time we were incredibly grateful to have been welcomed into their home.

That evening we went out with them again, this time to a local mall with a food court. We had dinner there.

It looked like any small mall in most North American cities. The only obvious differences were the food on the menus and that all the products — which looked like the ones in North America — had Thai writing. There was a large cosmetics store just inside the mall. I really was astonished.

We — or at least I — felt like a fish on display. There weren't many Caucasians around this area of Thailand. Walking through the mall was a unique experience considering it was fairly Americanized but everything was in Thai language. They even had a makeup stand and a food court: fast food Thai-style.

Nok and Sonchai did some grocery shopping and Bernie and I wandered around being lookie-loos.

Our hosts had a station wagon and the kids lay down in the back after dinner at the food court in the mall. After arriving back "home" we all went upstairs to watch a funny program on TV. We were really immersing ourselves into a brief glimpse of Thai life for blue-collar working families. We could never thank them enough for the hospitality shown to us, a couple from Canada they just met a day or two ago.

We got up early and had breakfast with Sonchai and the twins in the bright, welcoming kitchen. Nok was doing a morning shift at the local hospital. As we drank bodum after bodum of excellent coffee he spoke to us about challenges faced by teachers and students in Isaan.

Parents expected children — no demanded — he said, that children advance to the next grade whether or not they passed all classes.

There were no consequences if a student didn't do the work expected.

The teacher's salaries were very low, especially in the rural areas. At the time of this trip, the salary of 20,000 *baht* per month or approximately $750 Canadian dollars per month had not been raised for years. Of course, to us North Americans that sounded like a pathetically low income, but to us many products in Thailand were cheap. Eating out was inexpensive — again from our privileged point of view.

I didn't really understand the apathy from many of the teachers, parents, and school board. The whole school system in the rural communities needed an overhaul. How were any of these kids learning in the apathetic school system in rural Thailand?

These rural schools did not receive anywhere near the amount of supplies needed to properly teach. Some teachers were dedicated to teaching the children but many didn't take it seriously at all. Some would go home for lunch and not return later. With poor pay and very little school supplies it wasn't a wonder why.

We finished our breakfast — which was running into lunch — when Nok returned. We were all going out again.

We were having an interesting time communicating. Nok spoke French and Thai, and maybe other languages, but unfortunately not English. I had to stretch my brain to speak the French which I learned in school in Canada; it helped that I had lived in Ottawa and my two best friends were French-Canadian, so I picked up some that way too.

First, we needed to stop by a small local village and drop Nok off to see any patients in need of health care. Most clinics were few and far between, especially in the most rural of areas. I admired Nok for her dedication to nursing and provision of healthcare, especially to pregnant women and children in the rural villages that had no hospital close by.

Nok wasn't there long; she just needed to see two patients. So, back into the station wagon and away we went again.

It was spring break for the kids and there was a local agricultural fair. We drove there but I ended up walking with my cane around the fair. I was so happy that I was feeling strong enough to walk without having to go in my wheelchair.

There was a very large field of sunflowers in full bloom. Sunshine upon sunshine. I had never seen so many sunflowers in one spot ever. (I have seen them since, however, as they are grown in the valley where we now live.) There were also huge mountains of termites at the end of the field. One could sled down these hills of termite saliva dung and clay.

We took a ride on a wagon pulled by a trailer and saw some farm animals. My favourite spot was the orchid area. There were so many types of orchids I lost count. They were hanging in rafters and on poles, their aerial roots sprouting about looking like tentacles reaching for water and sunlight.

Our friends brought us some food. The chicken skewer looked good and I had already eaten half before I realized the meat near the bone was still pink. Considering everyone else was eating the food I didn't think about whether or not I should be eating it too. We had eaten in many restaurants and small street vendors on both trips and I had never had a problem with my stomach so I wasn't too concerned.

That evening we were going to dinner at a local restaurant where we would meet the VIP Stationery Guy who would be the man managing the school supplies. He was an important man in this area but I never really got his position straight.

We went back "home" to have a rest before going out for dinner later in the evening. We hopped into the station wagon, the kids in the back and drove to the restaurant where we were led to a long table in the back.

We waited awhile for the gentleman that we were to meet but he was running late. So we ordered some items as appetizers. The food was so very tasty. Finally after an hour of waiting Sonchai went again to phone Mr. Stationery and bad news — he couldn't make it. Well damn it, would have been nice to know a bit earlier. My energy definitely was depleted in the evenings and I could have used a rest. Mr. Stationery asked us to meet him at the same time the next night. The meeting he was in had gone way overtime and he apologized. Ok, we really wanted to meet this valuable contact, especially to ask questions, of which we had many. He also cancelled the following night.

We returned to Nok, Sonchai, and their twin's home and spent another evening in the twin bed (not with the twins, they had their own beds). And of course we were serenaded by the neighbour's yappy dog late into the evening and again early morning. I love animals but I was getting close to shouting out the window to get the critter to give us some peace. Didn't that little yappy thing never sleep?

My grandmother used to say that company was like fish, after three days they stink. We hoped that wasn't the case and there was no indication we were in the way. We were up early the next morning again. This time when I went down the stairs to the kitchen I missed the last two steps; it was dark I and twisted my ankle. Just what I didn't need. It did swell up some but I could walk in my sandals.

This was our last evening in Sisaket so we were hoping to finally meet Mr. Stationery at the same restaurant we were at a couple of evenings ago.

He did arrive, a little late, but he came all the same.

We discussed our charity plan with him. He was very open to listening and talked about all the schools in Isaan, and there were a lot. We would raise the money in Canada and send it to him to purchase additional supplies for each school.

We told him we would need to set up accounts with each school and would need the numbers and names of contacts, etc. He seemed interested. Really, why would he say no? The money would be going straight through his stationery supply business. Hmmm. At the time I didn't know how to feel about that but we thought with proper financial oversight we could make it work.

Our dinner was delicious again. I even ate little fried fish with the head and tail attached. They were crispy, like chips. I liked the way food was usually ordered in

Thailand when there were more than one or two people. Several different items were ordered and it was a treat eating all kinds of exotic foods.

We had achieved our goal of meeting a key person, Mr. Stationery, to talk about our charity and introduce ourselves. That was a good meeting. We now had hopes that our charity, *Thais That Bind*, could actually come to fruition.

CHAPTER 28

Korat Silk Factories

A different language is another version of life.
— Federico Fellini

The next morning we said our heartfelt thanks to our hosts and headed to Korat and the silk area. I had thought of another enterprise for us to pursue: buying Thai silk to sell in Canada.

We took a bus to Korat; it was a really good ride in a large clean tourist bus. We found a small hotel to stay in, and again it was difficult to find any English-speaking people. I was so glad we had taken the time to meet weekly with our translator back home.

We rented a small motorbike and toured around. The next day we set out on a highway where we were told there were some silk factories. My husband was brave to be driving a motorbike here in Korat, but we actually made out just fine.

The street signs from Korat to the silk factories were clear enough to understand when there was a stop sign or a yield sign. We did have to stop once and ask a traffic cop if we were on the right road and seek further directions to the silk factories. He actually understood our Thai and we understood his directions just fine.

We were able to walk through the factories and watch the process of dying and weaving the beautiful silk. The colours were astoundingly gorgeous. However, there was at least one younger boy in his mid-teens who had his bare hands in the dye vat. I didn't know if they used natural dyes or if the dye was toxic but it just didn't look safe.

The weavers were fast and every step of the process was by hand. Silk worms were grown in the hills in Korat and other regions.

We found a silk store near the factory, but without anyone speaking English we really couldn't get our questions answered. Oh well, importing silk looked like it might be a challenging undertaking, so we bought a few meters of silk to take home for personal use.

We only stayed a couple of nights in Korat; we wanted to get back to Bangkok and then further south to the beaches at Koh Samui, which sounded like heaven to me.

A critter in the form of a huge spider decided to park itself in the bathroom. I did not like snakes and I definitely didn't like spiders. Small ones or daddy-long-leg spiders were fine but encountering a spider as big as my palm, well that was really pushing my comfort zone. I wanted to keep one eye open all night but my exhaustion took over. The monster spider disappeared in the night and I didn't want to know where it went.

We took a long bus ride from Korat to Bangkok but again it was a smooth ride. Ten times better than any train we had taken.

We found our way back to the Kasseri Hotel in Bangkok and rested there for two nights. My stomach was starting to give me a bit of grief but it wasn't anything drastic, some nausea and loose stool but definitely manageable. We'd been eating a lot of fruit and a lot of strange food that my stomach had not ever have experienced, and it was protesting.

We often liked to take a tuk-tuk around Bangkok to go to the main spots we wanted to visit. One tuk-tuk driver had Tourette's syndrome, a condition where the afflicted have tics or twitches that cause unintended movements or outbursts of sound.

We had had so many bizarre events that this situation fit right in. Bernie barely fit in a tuk-tuk having such long legs: then add the wheelchair in and it was squishy. Both of Bernie's legs and the wheelchair wheels hung over the sides.

Now this guy with Tourette's syndrome was a ferocious driver. He zigged and zagged all over the road lanes, popping into any spot of space between cars or trucks all the while jerking his arms and legs and sputtering unknown words at everything. I do not know how we didn't get clipped by any vehicle around us. The situation was hilarious and not hilarious at the same time. Maybe the driver didn't care if he lived or died but we did. Life was very hard for many in Thailand. The poor guy was probably just trying to make as much money as he could with his rapid transportation of riders. The problem was that while he was well-seated in the front seat, Fred's legs could have been removed by passing vehicles. He finally got his legs inside the tuk-tuk by doing contortions; his knees were now in front of his face. We didn't go far.

Another day we set out and signalled for a tuk-tuk again. We still had many places we wanted to visit. We maneuvered ourselves into the small passenger bench behind the driver. I was pumped up; this would be our last hurrah in Bangkok. There really was so much to see and experience in a country so far removed from what our reality was like back home.

This driver had a cold — no, not just a cold but either whooping cough or pneumonia or who-the-heck-knows-what. It was a productive cough that cut his oxygen off. He seemed half-dead and kept hacking phlegm onto the road and probably sprayed it back onto us. After a five-minute ride we tapped him on the shoulder to indicate we wanted off. He was surprised, as our destination was much farther. Bernie handed him a significant amount of money, more than he would make in a day, or even a week. We tried to tell him to go home and get better. This driver needed to be off the streets. He might have done that, or he might have continued taking passengers and infecting hundreds with whatever virus he was carrying. Thoughts of our last trip contracting whooping cough were front and centre in our minds. We certainly didn't want to ever go through that nastiness again.

A couple of days later we flew to Koh Samui. A beautiful island off the Gulf of Thailand, which had grown over the years as tourists flock to the beautiful white sand beaches and warm turquoise waters.

We rented a small cabana directly on the beach. Bart set up his hammock on the porch and again we were in heaven. Again we rented a scooter to get around the island. There was so much to see.

CHAPTER 29

The End is Near

Beyond that time of my near death experience, that innate fear of death we all seem to be born with, just vanished.

— Rev. Craig Darling

One of our adventure days on the bike almost became our last day, and not just of the trip. Both of us must have at least nine lives, like cats, due to the many events that could have turned deadly — especially when travelling.

As Dan Simmons said in Entropy's Bed at Midnight, "Accidents are like death. Waiting for us everywhere. Unavoidable. Plan as we might, they defy our planning."

We were on another day of exploration on the back of a 150cc motorbike, not very big or powerful but it got us around where we wanted to be. We were coming back down a windy, narrow street. We were driving on the left side of the road as we should. Toward the bottom of the street the road took a sharp right. There was a road mirror for each side of the traffic to glance and check if anyone was approaching from the opposite direction and take caution.

Suddenly, we heard a big screech as a large white pick-up truck came careening around the corner at top speed. The driver, a Caucasian guy, bounced off the cement wall taking out his mirror and damaging the passenger side of the new-looking truck. But that bang didn't stop him; he gunned the truck up the road toward us. I sat horrified behind Bernie on the small motorbike and we thought we were about to die or be severely injured. There was a ditch to our left but it was a drop far enough down to really bang us up hard. There was nowhere to go. My heart was in my mouth, visions of my kids flashed through my head. *Not again!*

Suddenly Bernie gunned the small bike; we flew over the corner of the ditch and barely landed on a driveway as the truck passed within inches of us. We were both shaking pretty badly. There were people around that witnessed the whole event but nobody came to see if we were ok. The truck carried on. Some drunken tourist nearly took us out. Idiot.

According to my travel diary I had many flashbacks of the truck speeding toward us, especially in my dreams. The image makes me shudder still. Another event to add to my PTSD.

Later that evening about six, back at our bungalow, it was peaceful and quiet. People were out for dinner. I sat and listened to the beach sounds, looking at the beautiful sparkling water and the white foamy waves that were crashing onto the beach. The sunsets were much more brilliant on the west side of Thailand than in Koh Lanta, but I did prefer the water here in Koh Samui. The weather had been cloudy off and on, but very hot and humid.

The next day I was exhausted: probably the adrenaline coming down after the too-close-for-comfort truck incident. I spent the day sleeping off and on. I felt very wiped out And I had horrible deep aching pain.

The previous several nights there had been an outdoor festival nearby. It started mid-afternoon and carried on until one in the morning. How did anybody sleep? Some people ran businesses and must have had to be up early. The last two hours each evening there was a good band playing. Free entertainment. We didn't mind.

I got my nerve up and we went for another bike ride the next day. This time we went rural and stayed away from touristy areas. I was glad we did, it was always a treat exploring what the country was really like everywhere. There were many empty partially-built high rises and empty gated homes. There was a lot of cleared land for sale. This was one year after the 2008 financial crisis and many companies didn't't survive. Only Thais can purchase land, but deals can be made through marriage of a Thai citizen, or sometimes financial partnership.

I was really sore after our too-long ride the other day. Taking a day or two off in between strenuous activities was the ticket to keeping me comfortable.

We ate lunch on the beach. There were vendors there, hauling their wares. One guy turned up every afternoon carrying two large metal containers over his neck like a yoke. It looked burdensome. It was a propane grill of sorts and he could grill up BBQ chicken or corn and pineapple. All of the Thais we had seen worked very hard and we were always happy when he showed up so we could have some very juicy pineapple and mango. My mouth got blisters from eating so much fruit but I've never had pineapple, papaya, or mango anywhere close to the sweet, rich mouth dripping fruit here. I want to go back now just to taste that lovely fruit.

Our time in Thailand would soon be ending; we had just a few more days.

We decided to take a passenger ferry to the next island over: we could see it from the beach. The island, Koh Phangan, was small and had a forty-kilometre perimeter. It was where the famous Full Moon Party is held, on the small beach at Haad Rin. The monthly all-night event attracted anywhere from 10,000 to 30,000 people, mostly tourists. When I saw the beach where this party was held I couldn't believe it could hold anywhere close to that amount of people. Drugs and booze rock the night, scantily clad young-uns party hard — what could possibly go wrong? I looked it up and it wasn't pretty. There was a horrible bus accident that killed fourteen tourists one year. The roads were narrow and there were several hairpin turns. You didn't want to be driving this tiny island drunk or stoned. Like I said: what could possibly go wrong? But now I'm sounding like my grandma.

We weren't going to be there during the Full Moon Party, which was fine. The island was busy enough without tens of thousands more tourists.

The passenger ferry was full and it was a pleasant cruise. After we landed I waited at a table on an outdoor patio, of which there were many up and down the street, both ground-floor and upper-story patios. They also seemed fairly full with happy people.

Bernie was renting a scooter, along with several other people, so we could explore the whole island. There were some beautiful water lilies floating in the pond beside me on the restaurant patio where I waited: such a perfect flower.

The road was definitely dangerous at times with narrow switchbacks and almost no sides to the road before big drop-offs. Steep roads, but the view of the clear turquoise sea below, sparkling like a million stars, was spectacular. I had loved Hawaii but this little island was like the beautiful parts of the Hawaiian Islands on steroids, without the huge high rises that looked like they could topple Honolulu into the ocean.

I truly had never seen such beauty. I would have relocated here in a heartbeat but there were snakes: great big hungry, horrible snakes. I'd tried to — if not like snakes — then at least ignore the fact that Thailand had huge deadly snakes and carry on. Snakes didn't like me either so hopefully we could maintain our own boundaries.

I loved this little island all the same. There were a few beautiful little places for sale on a nice plot of land but I was sure that if I actually lived there, I might become tired of the heavy traffic (at least near the town), the many inebriated tourists that could cause fights, over-doses or other health emergencies, especially on the Full Moon Party nights. It wasn't like there were any hospitals nearby. Plus there were snakes. I do not like snakes, did I already mention that? Perhaps if they were furry and didn't try to strangle or poison me then maybe we'd get along better.

There were many beaches — up to twenty — around the small island; the ones we stopped at were incredibly beautiful. The words escape me; how to describe paradise? It filled me with joy and peace. It was a perfect moment in my life. I took many pictures but they didn't capture the emotions of the scene.

The road rose steeply outside of Haad Rin. I held on for dear life to as we climbed the hill. I was still a bit shaky from our near crash a few days before. However, the scenery was some of the best of our trip. There were several resorts around the island with bungalows, some on stilts. It all looked so tranquil, it would be nice to return someday and stay a few weeks.

Although most of Thailand's elephants were for tourist events, we saw several clearing logs from a forest. They were working hard. I was surprised because logging was banned in 1989. Maybe they weren't logging but clearing and piling logs for some reason I couldn't quite figure out. It looked like the land was being scraped for some development of sorts. Some poor dude was about to lose his little one-room shack right at the edge of the field. Or maybe he got to stay. It was a tin lean-to, but inhabited.

We sat on a lovely beach, Salad Beach I believe. We had a tasty lunch — not salad — and a beer and were entertained by a fire dancer. He spoke with us later and showed us his many burn marks but seemed proud by how much he had learned through practice.

Sadly, we left the island but were lucky to take the ferry back to Koh Samui just as the sun was setting: it was such beauty: sparkling orange, red, and purple sunset beams glittering on the sea like rubies, diamonds, amethysts and citrine. Jewels of the sea.

Goodbye paradise. I still marvel at that absolutely perfect day.

Two nights later was the full moon. The day before the full moon I had noticed the water had gone murky. The water had been warm and very clear like bath water. Now it looked like a plow had gone through the water, churning up the muck.

I went in the water the day after the full moon. The water was definitely turbid. There was a group of kids from the local school for foreigners, having a swimming lesson nearby.

I wanted to have a good swim before we had to leave for home. I still wasn't able to swim far after I got sick; this was so frustrating for me as that was a weekly activity of mine that I loved before I was forced to stop working and doing sports.

I was doing the breaststroke when suddenly my chest started hurting. It felt like I was being electrocuted. Maybe I was having a heart attack. I tried to swim back to the shore which wasn't far, but the electric shocks stopped me in my tracks. I was finally able to stand up and saw shreds of white mucous trails in the water.

I didn't know that it was a jellyfish. The kids were still in the water not far away from me but I was clutching my stomach, and my right arm was burning so much I couldn't shout out; all I could do was run into our bungalow and go straight under the cold shower.

Finally Bernie came back from using the internet. When he saw the pain I was in and heard what had happened he ran to the small outdoor restaurant to find vinegar. He had recently emptied his bladder so the "traditional" method of spraying urine on the jellyfish burns wasn't going to happen — plus it's an old wives tale.

There wasn't any vinegar, or the restaurant workers didn't understand what he was asking for. They probably had something similar they used for cooking but we didn't ever learn the Thai word for vinegar.

I stood under the cold shower for a long time until the burning pain lessened.

I had a fifteen centimetre burn mark on my upper stomach near my heart and another ten centimeter burn line on the inside of my right arm. It definitely could have been worse. I had been stung by the toxin-filled mucus strings that jellyfish shed into the water to stun nearby creatures or as a reaction when jellyfish are startled.

I was really happy we were leaving for home the next day. My stomach was in dire straits, with nausea and some diarrhea and the burning sting from the jelly fish, but I thought that my upset tummy might be from all the juicy, delicious pineapple we'd been eating every day. My jelly fish stings were long red lines plus a lot of smaller burns scattered on my torso and arm. It was very painful for weeks.

We packed our bags and said goodbye to beautiful Thailand and its people.

CHAPTER 30

The Diagnosis

> *With a strange logic, [Rod Liddle] asserts that because ME patients deny that they have a psychiatric disorder, this proves they have a psychiatric disorder.*
> *Meanwhile, people are quietly dying of ME. ME sufferer Emily Collingridge died, aged 30; Victoria Webster died at just 18. People don't die from 'exercise phobia.' ME is not 'lethargy' and 'aches and pains' as Liddle claims. Severe ME is lying in a darkened room, alone, in agonizing pain, tube-fed, catheterized, and too weak to move or speak.*
> — Tanya Marlow

It's always nice to travel but sleeping in your own bed is like that first shower after having a baby or after hiking for a few days without amenities.

I certainly didn't feel well at all once we got home. I was exhausted, nauseated, and vomited at least once a day. What was going on this time? I had a sneaky feeling it was the not fully-cooked chicken at the Agrifair. I was losing weight and had lost my appetite.

Off to the doctor I went and after several blood tests it showed I had a campylobacter infection. I was put on heavy-duty antibiotics which didn't stop it the first time, so I went on a second round of antibiotics. I met a young man at the rehab pool I attended. He had contracted the same campylobacter bacteria, but as with any virus or bacteria it could damage nerves and organs. He became a quadriplegic as a result of the infection.

Five months later I felt back to my "normal" self, which really wasn't what I felt was normal for anyone my age.

Over the next couple of years I kept losing weight. I was not a big person to begin with, I tried to eat as much as possible but my weight kept going down. I'd always thought I was overweight, thanks to my mother. One of the first things she said to me after I gave birth to my second child was "It looks like you need to lose some weight." Really mother, that's what's on your mind just hours after delivering my baby over a month early?

So I'd never seen my body as anything but chunky, until I lost so much weight I was down to eighty-three pounds. Then I got scared. I had become the disappearing woman.

I had a new doctor attending me, my regular one was on stress leave. Fortunately, this new doctor listened to me and took my symptoms very seriously. She sent me on an urgent visit to the Rapid Assessment Clinic at one of the large hospitals in Vancouver.

I was finally diagnosed with Central Sensitivity Syndrome. Now that diagnosis I could accept and understand.

Before I was able to get into the Chronic Complex Disease Program in Vancouver, I kept getting sicker and sicker. Noises bothered me, bright lights bothered me, and I had swollen glands, nausea and vomiting, and a sore throat off and on. I felt like I had a constant flu weighing me down, exhausting me day after day.

I had been off all opioids but along with losing weight rapidly I also had a lot more pain. At one point the pain was so incredible I could hardly speak. I was stuck in bed and would yelp in pain if I even moved an inch. My dear husband had to bring me a slipper-style bedpan to use as I couldn't even get up from the bed to a commode.

I refused to be taken to the local emergency room for many reasons, one being I had just seen a woman on TV speaking about her terrible treatment at this hospital. I knew the doctor she was talking about. I'd had issues with him over the years and he was finally let go after an angry letter from me — and I'm sure others — to the hospital administrator.

I thought I was dying. I had never had such pain. Chronic pain can't be compared with acute pain. I knew the pain of labour and delivery, but the pain I was experiencing was worse because it was there day after day after day, whereas at the end of labour and delivery I had a wonderful happy outcome which helped alleviate the pain. Even with a broken leg, the expected outcome is "getting back to normal". Not so with chronic pain conditions. There may be some ok days with less pain, but the pain is always there, like an unwanted friend or relative you have to put up with.

"Make pain your friend," one well-meaning writer has said. You have got to be kidding me; pain had never been my friend. It exhausted me. I hated it. With friends like that who needs enemies?

The pain did settle after several weeks and I was accepted into the Chronic Complex Disease Program in Vancouver BC. I was hoping my diagnosis would be clearer. I had been doing a lot of research on medical journals online and my symptoms kept adding up to a medical condition I didn't know much about, or had ever heard about: myalgic encephalomyelitis or ME/CFS.

I was put on medication that increased my craving for food significantly. I learned that I was sensitive to gluten and lactose. The less carbs I ate the better I felt. I found that increasing my protein and B vitamins helped stop sugar and carb cravings: if I could make it three days without high carbs and sugar, my cravings completely went away. However, I enjoy food, and staying on a strict diet goes out the window at Christmastime or my birthday, and when we travel. So whenever those events happen I have to start all over again.

After filling out the reams of questionnaires which included every symptom I had, I definitely had myalgic encephalomyelitis (ME/CFS) plus fibromyalgia. ME/CFS is a complex disease that can affect every system in your body.

To this day I still do not know if fibromyalgia is related to ME, or if ME is severe fibromyalgia.

There are millions of ME/CFS patients around the world. There are over a million people in Canada alone who have ME, fibromyalgia, Lyme disease or multiple chemical sensitivities. There are people who have ME who are able to work part-time but the majority of patients are house or bed-bound, sometimes for years on end. Children have been taken away from their families and forcibly committed to a psychiatric unit. This is NOT a psychiatric disease. All the counselling in the world will not impact myalgic encephalomyelitis. Counselling may help the patient come to terms with a devastating, life altering medical condition. It might help the patient learn to meditate and listen to their body, but it will not ever cure anyone with ME/CFS.

Patients need to be diagnosed quickly and put on modified activities of daily life. The more rest the body and mind have, the higher chance there is of regaining some, or most, of the patient's energy level.

Unfortunately most patients are either not taken seriously, or they are encouraged to keep exercising to maintain muscle mass and strength. ME is a paradox. Patients may try to get better by regular strengthening programs, but activity makes ME much worse. Every person with ME has a limited amount of energy to get through the day. Think of energy as a commodity, a piggy bank with a few pennies in. Some people have more, but others less. Most people can spend some or all of them doing activities and they are topped up at night. But most people with ME don't get quality sleep so they also spend some of those pennies during the night.

Most of us with ME have spent most of our pennies just getting up and dressed. So the remainder of the day we're broke. ME feels like you have run a marathon every day.

Pacing is key to managing this disease. People with ME know how many pennies they have in their piggy bank and get by each day exerting small bits of energy. But life is life and there's always something that occurs — either physically or mentally, especially when not expected — that takes all the pennies away and can take days, weeks, or months to replenish the pennies in the piggy bank.

I know I'm going to spend most of my pennies when I meet my friends for lunch or spend time with my grandkids, but I try to rest as much as possible before and after these events. Sometimes it doesn't work out the way I hoped and it takes much longer to collect my pennies again. This is why most friends or relatives don't see the true picture of what happens after our pennies are spent. We crash, usually at home. For me that means increased deep-muscle pain, nerve pain that feels like toothpicks are being jammed up my fingers, nausea, sweating at the drop of a hat, and exhaustion.

Some low-dose antidepressants and off-label drugs may help with pain somewhat, but it is far from a cure. I know when I am clinically depressed and I know when I'm not, and I definitely know the difference. Doctors need not be so cavalier with many unseen functional diseases like fibromyalgia and myalgic encephalomyelitis. Just because things like inflammation and levels of pain can't be seen, doesn't mean they aren't there. They are. But until advanced diagnostics are invented and made mainstream, please don't tell me "It's all in my head." In 2017, Stats Canada published a report that showed that fibromyalgia and ME patients have some of the highest unmet medical needs. There is a lot of misinformation about this disease. I regularly go to a few online medical resources to keep up with research from all over the world. In 2021, Tracy White and the head geneticist at Stanford University, Dr. Ron Davis, wrote a book about Davis' son Whitney DaFoe. DaFoe has had ME for many years. He was a young man struck down in his late twenties: a world traveller and photojournalist. His story has also appeared in many articles and online platforms. There are doctors, nurses, scientists, athletes — the list of people affected by ME goes on and on. It can affect any age group. There are no concrete diagnostic tools although some are being worked on. There are no treatments that change one's health status significantly, just pacifiers.

Now we're enduring a pandemic. However, a virus such as Covid-19 will not go quietly. Unfortunately, some people who contracted this disease before vaccinations were available, or those who don't have enough immunity from the vaccines (or those who refuse vaccinations) will still be sick months or years later. Scientists are finding a lot of similarities between ME/CFS and long-haul Covid sufferers. The recent attention paid to this makes many of us who have had ME for decades feel ignored but hopefully science will eventually link the two conditions. Dr. Fauci, the former Chief Medical Advisor in the United States has spoken about the similarities between long-haul Covid 19 and myalgic encephalomyelitis or ME/CFS.

CHAPTER 31

Life as Kat

Another purpose in life goes down the drain
— KI

Coming to terms with a disability does not happen overnight nor does it happen smoothly.

We tried to keep the charity, *Thais That Bind*, alive once we got home from our second trip to Thailand, but it was a lot harder than it seemed to have committed board members, let alone raise money for a brand-new unknown charity. I was so exhausted every day it was impossible to carry on. We had to dissolve our attempt to help the school kids on the other side of the world.

Life as Kathryn is like watching a car wreck over and over. My kids constantly tell me to enclose myself in bubble wrap.

My clumsiness has become worse over the years. ME causes brain inflammation and that alone affects all sorts of issues with balance, digestion, blood pressure, and so much more. I get diplopia or double vision which gets worse if I'm overtired or in an energy crash with increased symptoms. The double vision seems to be due to my eye muscles that control the pupils: the muscles may not be getting enough energy from the cells to function properly.

This past year alone I've fallen hard three times. The first time I was walking our dogs across the street behind the houses, where there's a beautiful creek surrounded by trees. A few times I've seen bear and deer wandering up the creek. It isn't a long walk but the trail is up and down. In one spot I need to hold onto a tree branch and pull myself up the incline and around the tree. I'm super wary if I walk by that incline.

It was the end of July and we were leaving in less than a week on our yearly vacation to Kelowna, BC where my oldest son, wife, and my youngest granddaughter live. The dogs were hot and so was I. I often let them off leash, if no other animals are around and they go down a short hill to the water for a drink and a lay down.

I started down the hill as I have done many times. But I had flip-flop sandals on. I realized after I'd already left the house that I hadn't changed them to more supportive sandals or shoes.

As I started down the three foot hill, I caught my toes under a root that was partly above ground but most underneath. "Oh shit" I said to absolutely no one but the dogs. I landed on river rocks a few inches from the water. I laid there afraid to move. I kept fainting but finally became alert enough to get my injured foot into the cold water. I splashed cold water on my face over and over to stay conscious.

Both dogs came to my side and stayed. Too bad they couldn't have used my cell phone to call for help. My glasses were full of dirt and water, so was the front of my cell phone. Thank goodness I always brought it along, just in case.

I kept getting dizzy and had to wait until my head cleared enough to wipe my glasses and phone. I didn't want to call 911 as I didn't know how the emergency workers would find me, I wasn't thinking straight. Also what about the dogs? I doubted the emergency team would take them along in an ambulance. So I called my husband: my knight in shining armour. I was able to describe where I was and waited twenty minutes while he drove to the location from work. The dogs heard him calling before I did, and they bounded up the trail to lead him to me.

I tried a few times to put pressure on my ankle but it was too painful. I even tried scooting up the incline backwards but that didn't work. My knight threw me over his shoulder and hauled me up the incline and bushwhacked his way to the road. He took me to the local emergency where I waited four hours to be seen and processed. I had broken my ankle and it took nearly a year to heal.

I missed our annual trip to the Okanagan but considering we had entered into a deadly pandemic it may have been best for me to stay home. But I wasn't at all happy about the injury.

The previous spring I had cut my finger on a blender blade while making my protein shake for breakfast. As a nurse I've seen plenty of blood and many other things that would cause a person to faint, and I didn't normally faint.

But ever since I had pneumonia twenty years previous, fainting had become part of my life.

That morning I did: I fainted right on the kitchen floor. The dogs came running over and I came to a bit, but as I tried to get to my cell phone which was on a table, I fainted again. This went on for twenty minutes.

Finally, I was able to reach a phone, fainted again, and got in touch with Bernie who came to my rescue one more time. That took another twenty minutes, so I had been lying on the floor for forty minutes. As advertised with *I've fallen and I can't get up!* we did buy an alarm for me to wear but I lost it somewhere in the house. Occasionally we'd hear it but could never find it. I know I really should get another one.

I don't want to sit at home and do nothing at all. I realize I'm a walking disaster — I will take a bubble-wrapped coat along like the kids suggested.

There have been so many interesting, challenging, and life-threatening events in my life that I'm quite surprised I'm still here on earth.

I don't know why life can be such a rollercoaster for some but not others.

I don't know why I was struck down midlife when I had so much more I wanted to do. I did lose my purpose.

How does one find a purpose when disability keeps you down? I don't know from one day to the next how much energy or pain I will have.

I asked my eldest son one Christmas, late at night after some bottles of wine, what he thought having a purpose in life meant. His answer, similar to Eleanor Roosevelt's quote, was to live. Simple as that.

I've taken that answer to heart. I live.

There have been a few times over the years I have come face to face with the possibility of my early demise. Whether it was the time I was attacked in Hawaii, close-calls on trips while on a scooter, or the level of pain and exhaustion I could no longer cope with, I looked at the possibility I could no longer carry on. But who would that serve?

I would devastate my husband, kids, and grandkids if I were to exit this life prematurely.

Yes I suffer. Lots of people suffer.

Buddha said "Life is suffering," and for many people around the world suffering is life.

There are so many things I want to do but when I think about the actual doing of the thing I realize how exhausted and in pain I am.

I watch chefs on a couple of talk shows and I would love to make these meals to give Bernie a break, but most days I have just enough energy to walk the dogs, which at least gets me out of the house and into the green.

I get excited at Christmastime and summer vacation to be with my kids and grandkids. I save my energy for a week before such events because I know I always crash afterwards.

I can run on adrenaline for only so long. Many times I try to convince myself to just keep going, to keep up the higher energy pace. To be a Forrest Gump. I often delude myself wishing and hoping I'll be out of pain and get my energy and life back if I just keep going, but no. Every time I try to increase my endurance, even taking baby steps to increase my function, I collapse.

I'm always covered in bruises, aside from my falls. I have poor balance. My head often feels like I just got off a boat and I'm still swaying on the ocean waves. My arms and legs look like a Jackson Pollock painting in shades of purple, blue, and red.

Nowadays, I must pace myself carefully, although there will be times when I happily push myself beyond my usual limits, knowing I'll probably crash later but that the event will be worth it.

My day is scheduled and needs to remain that way as much as possible.

I get up around 8:30. I feed the dogs and myself, then I sit on my recliner until eleven or noon. I practice online Spanish which helps keep my brain active. After lunch I drive somewhere within half an hour from home and walk the dogs, carefully, in several beautiful spots around Chilliwack. I need to be outdoors every day. I need to breathe deeply and feel the air. I love the green: we live in a rainforest. I love the fields full of corn or cows and horses nearby. When the sun is out I marvel at the nearby mountains full of snow from late fall to spring. They decorate our skyline from Vancouver to the Fraser Valley. We can see the Cheam Range from the back of our house and last year Bernie hired a helicopter to take me for a flight of a lifetime for my milestone birthday. We flew around Cheam and down to the Cascade Mountains which eventually go south to Washington, Oregon, and Northern California. I'm so thankful to live in such a beautiful location.

Bernie and I rarely go out for dinner as I'm just too exhausted by four in the afternoon. Thankfully he's a great cook and I usually do the clean-up the next morning after rinsing them the night before: Mom would literally be horrified if she knew but who cares? It isn't like we have people drop in for coffee and if they do, well, tough luck.

I'm usually in bed by 7:00, practice more Spanish, and read for a couple of hours then fall asleep by 10:00. I cannot sit upright for more than an hour or I get dizzy, stomach pain and I'm much more exhausted.

I seem to sleep for an hour or two then awake for a few hours, then back to sleep for my deepest sleep from 4:00 to 8:00.

Every day I feel like I've run a twenty-kilometre marathon, plus worked a twelve-hour night shift. I'm often nauseated in the morning and get sore throats and swollen glands. I feel like a pregnant woman running a marathon.

I'm exhausted, exhausted, exhausted.

I used to go to a women's book club once a month in the afternoon, and they often met for lunch first. There were more times than not where I didn't make it at all or either missed lunch or the book discussion. I also started a knitting and crochet club and held it at my place every two weeks for six months or so, then other women offered their places and we would take turns. Showing up every two weeks was a challenge but after twenty-plus years of not having friends I craved socialization. It backfired though. I got a lot worse. After two years of not going to meetings or restaurants due to Covid, my symptoms were much better, easier to manage than the previous years anyway but I continue with flare-ups or "crashes" as I call them..

I started "crashing" just before this past Christmas; I noticed I was getting very forgetful, more than usual, and stumbling over words. My pain level was very high and lying down in bed was excruciating, like lying on a bed of nails. My double vision had gotten a lot worse over the past six months. I've been getting horrible headaches. When I crash I get increased brain inflammation and my anxiety level goes sky high; I get hot and cold sweats, my heart feels like it's pounding, I can barely eat and I have little energy. When I stretch my arms or legs it feels like they are shattering or oxygenated blood is not reaching them. They tingle and feel like I've way over exercised and have a buildup of lactic acid in all of my muscles.

Due to the Covid-19 pandemic, we haven't travelled to another country since returning back to Vancouver from Vegas just a few days before the world shut down. Bernie has been talking about travelling after his last big work project at work before he retires: I just hope I can travel again. I have to be at a higher functioning level to even consider a trip anywhere.

I constantly keep up with my ME friends across the globe via social media and read every new paper published by researchers on fibromyalgia and myalgic encephalomyelitis.

I follow a few researchers: one such man I have already mentioned, Ron Davis, is a professor of biochemistry and genetics and the Director of the Stanford Genome Technology Center. His son has ME and I've been following both men in the quest for answers to this confounding medical condition.

ME/CFS is a life-robbing disease. Never in my wildest dreams did I ever imagine my active happy life would change so drastically. I've had to "change my mind" as my

French brother-in-law used to say, and find other things in life to give me meaning. My life has gone from being a super busy, full-of-life, ready-for-action woman to a whisper.

In the past two years my new family doctor has put me through a lot of diagnostics to rule everything out that may be causing symptoms.

Of course every test proves to be negative. I have a good heart, lungs, kidneys and bowels (I do have irritable bowel syndrome, but no structural issues). I saw part of the cardiologists report at my family doctor's office. Again the "S" word. *Somatization* popped up from the page. I could have screamed. That cardiology stress test nearly did me in. I was holding onto the bars of the walker so hard I practically levitated. I couldn't let go to push the stop button or I would have gone flying backwards. I couldn't even speak Sure, I passed the cardiac test but my energy level plummeted drastically over the following three days and lasted nearly a month. If I had to do that test two days in a row, well, I'd fail. I never would have been able to even walk slowly. I couldn't even walk my dogs for a few weeks..

Every test was negative so that leaves the brain and nervous system. With conditions like ME and FM the central nervous system goes wonky, and is on high alert. One book I read on chronic pain suggested our brain functioning is like an out-of-tune orchestra or when musicians practice before a show. Some other hypotheses have been put out by researchers: the Glycolysis pathway that converts glucose as part of the energy conversion needed by the body's cells to function has broken down; another hypothesis is that we enter a hibernation state where, like the bear, our body almost shuts down to conserve energy. It's a puzzling disease.

Also, I have fibromyalgia, which causes horrible pain in many areas of the body. It can feel like you've been hit by a truck: everything hurts. Deep joint pain, needles poking down my fingers, sciatic pain, aching and stabbing.

Many nights I wake up with deep burning pain in my hips and shoulders. I spent two years with such pain and spasms in my lower back that I was walking around the house like Groucho Marx minus the cigar.

Over the past twenty years I've not seen any great advances in knowledge of FM or ME. There may be hypotheses but for many reasons the research doesn't pan out, often due to the lack of research money to continue studies. The powers that be in government have not been helpful enough, far too few people have ever heard of FM, let alone ME. They are invisible diseases and the majority of us don't have the ability to protest. We are too weak, bed-bound, or housebound. Some patients are young, school-aged children; some have been athletes; others are doctors or lawyers. This disease has the ability to affect any person on a long-term basis, often for life. Patients have ended their lives because there seems to be no hope for a diagnostic tool to clearly show whether one truly has these diseases, nor are there adequate treatments to make much of a difference in the patient's life. The constant exhaustion and pain would drive many people to call it quits. Living with ME/CFS is a very personal journey. Some patients only have five percent of normal functioning and remain bed-bound for years. Others like myself go from five to forty percent throughout the year.

I've learned to predict what will set me back. When I was down at my lowest, with the most severe pain and exhaustion, I was not really sure if I would be able to carry on with my life, so I have a lot of empathy for those who cannot.

I have a lot of concern for the future of many Covid-19 survivors; there are too many that will end up like me and millions of others around the world. A certain percentage of Covid patients will develop long-term symptoms very similar, if not the same, as people with ME/CFS. The long-term symptoms may be slightly different but generally there is extreme exhaustion, sleep disturbances, swollen glands, stomach issues, and brain fog; I could go on.

The lack of help and understanding regarding ME leaves a person grieving for their past healthy life. We have all felt ignored, criticized, abandoned, and left to ourselves to find our way.

Will the powers that be listen now?

I had an internal medicine/rheumatology specialist ask me recently how long I had been off work. "Twenty years," I said. Her reply was "What have you been doing all that time?"

"Living," I said.

Pain, exhaustion, and suffering,
A trio that always seems to bring,
A heaviness that's hard to bear,
A burden that's always there.
Days are a struggle, nights are long,
Every moment feels like a marathon,
The pain is like a fire that never stops,
The exhaustion a weight that never drops.
Attempts to explain this to others,
Is like trying to catch a ghost that hovers,
It's an invisible weight that no one can see,
But it's always there, haunting me.
Some days I push through the pain,
Other days it feels like I'm going insane,
But no matter how much I try to hide,
The suffering is always there, deep inside.
It's like living in a world of constant noise,
Where every sound is amplified and destroys,
The peace and quiet I so desperately crave,
Leaving me feeling lost, hopeless, and afraid.
But in the midst of this pain and despair,
I find strength in knowing I'm not alone in this affair,
There are others who are fighting too,
And together we'll make it through.
So though the pain and exhaustion linger,
I'll hold onto hope and become a singer,
Of a tune that speaks of courage, and grace,
And of a future where suffering has no place.

— KLI

PHOTOS FROM OUR TWO TRIPS TO THAILAND

A gas station

A little crowded

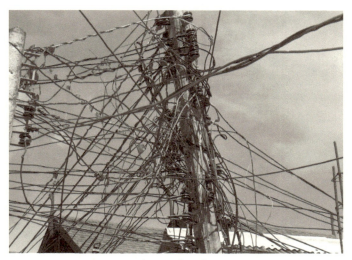

An electrical nightmare

Baby elephants

Buddhist Monks everywhere

Different Wat

Elephants everywhere

Entering the Elephant Festival

Festival of Lights; Loy Krathong

Floating Wat Koh Samui

Foster girl and friends

Glass bottle Wat

Hill Tribe woman

In a cafe

Koh Phangan full moon party island

Laying down Golden Buddha

Our cabana in Koh Samui

Our foster girl with family and friends

Our transportation

Putting on the brakes five min before departure

Regal Elephant

Sea Gypsies Koh Lanta

Silk factory

Small but pretty Wat

Somebody's house

Suring Elephant Festival

Thailand Visit with Nutjaree

The Aussie Monk

The Village

The whole family

Village woman

Walk around the village

Watching the tele from the porch

Wats everywhere

White Buddha Koh Samui

White Wat near the Mekong River

Working man

APPENDIX

Fibromyalgia symptoms:

Widespread pain and tender points
Problems with balance
Fatigue
Sleep disturbances
Morning stiffness
Brain fog/cognitive problems
Migraines/other headaches
Mood disorders
Overlapping conditions such as: Irritable Bowel Syndrome, Restless Leg Syndrome, Tinnitus, and more

ME/CFS symptoms:

Extreme exhaustion
Post-exertional malaise: an important hallmark of ME/CFS
Non-restorative sleep
Brain fog/cognitive impairment
Joint pain

Inflamed lymph nodes
Persistent sore throat
Severe headache
Neurological abnormalities
Complete organ system shutdown
Sensitivity to light, sound, odours, chemicals, foods, and medications
Irritability, depression, and mood swings

Resources:

Canadian Consensus Criteria on ME/CFS
Chronic Complex Disease Program in BC, Canada
Fukuda Criteria on ME/CFS
Health Rising blog: www.healthrising.org
Hummingbird Foundation for ME: www.hfme.org
International Consensus on ME/CFS
National ME/FM Action Network Ottawa Ontario: www.mefmaction.com
Open Medicine Foundation: www.omfcanada.ngo
Provincial groups: online

Works Cited:

Glimour, Heather and Jungwee Park. "Medically unexplained physical symptoms (MUPS) among adults in Canada." Statistics Canada, 2019, https://www150.statcan.gc.ca/n1/pub/82-003-x/2017003/article/14780-eng.htm

White, Tracie and Ron Davis. *The Puzzle Solver*. Legacy Lit, 2021

New Canadian Guidelines for Opioid 2017 for Non-Cancer Pain: Canadian Medical Association

ABOUT THE AUTHOR

The author, Kathryn Larouche Imler, is a retired registered nurse with a varied work background in general medicine, surgery, gynecology and obstetrics. After an injury, she left hospital nursing and worked as a nursing supervisor for home care. Kathryn's final job was an assistant director of care on a dementia/medical ward before becoming disabled due to a rare, almost unheard of medical condition which took nearly a decade to properly diagnose.

Kathryn continued to pursue research on her medical condition, Myalgic encephalomyelitis (ME) and fibromyalgia (FM) and has in-depth knowledge about these and other „unseen" medical conditions. There are millions of people around the world affected by fibromyalgia, ME/CFS, Lyme disease, GWS and many other conditions that are poorly understood by most of the medical profession. Ten percent of the net sales will go to support various societies involved in research for ME/CFS and FM.

Made in United States
Troutdale, OR
07/11/2023